Montana Made

HOW LOSING MY FATHER, MY MIND, AND MY PATIENCE MADE ME (SORT OF) A BETTER MAN

GARTH GERHART

LIBRARY TALES PUBLISHING

Published by Library Tales Publishing
www.librarytalespublishing.com

ISBN
9798894410333

First Edition, 2025
Printed in the United States of America

Thanks to Jenny for your heart, mind, love, and persistence.
You are my Guardian Angel. :)

FOR DAD

Contents

Preface

This book isn't a self-help book, but I hope you find it helpful. It chronicles my journey, and I aspire for it to assist you on yours.

I didn't realize how lost I was until I was gone. I hope you find inspiration here to discover your own path.

May you find your Montana.

Prologue

WHERE ARE YOU FROM?

"Where are you from?"

I HATE that question. Not really the question, but the absoluteness it entails and evokes. It's also an opening question that mostly fills in gaps when you're waiting for a better conversation to come around or making small talk with someone you'll hopefully never see again.

It can also be asked to lead into another question like, "What is it like there?" "How did you end up here?" "When was the last time you were there?" or the introspective question to themselves of, "Hmmm... who else do I know from there?"

I imagine that most people have these responses preloaded in their frontal cortex, where they store most interactions, and can recite them faster than their staple order at Starbucks. For me, and most military brats, the answers are never that simple.

Asking a brat where they are from usually elicits one of two responses. Some people have panic attacks as they scramble to go into a long-winded diatribe about where they were born, how and when they moved, where they moved, and how they repeated that process every three years. Once that genie is out of the bottle, it's followed by a slew of questions from an audience that wants to know everything about the cultures you've experienced and your worldly views. It's a context of geographical superiority, and I have enough issues feeling inadequate without comparing passports. Take it easy, guys; I put my Lederhosen on one leg at a time.

However, I can usually gauge my response based on the person. If it's someone I am trying to impress on a broad professional spectrum, I usually say, "Germany." If it's a respectable older white male, I will hop between "Colorado" or "Texas." If it's a POC, I usually go with "The South." If it's an attractive woman, I charm her (and subsequently disgust her) with, "Wherever you want me to be, Hot Pants."

Like most adults with my background, we just try our best to fit in. Whatever I say could be cross-checked, validated, and excused by the time I spent moving from place to place every few years. Growing up in the conditions I was born and raised in allowed me to slide easily into any place and role as I became more worldly and less attached to any place or time.

A unique talent that we also share is our ability to move on at record speed. By the time we settled into a new school, made new friends, and started a new life, we had to leave as quickly as we could prematurely ejaculate in our Z. Cavariccis. In fact, we usually had an opportunity to reinvent ourselves every few years as we, and the times, had changed.

When my stepfather's Army unit moved to Germany in 1990, I was able to take my awkward, geeky persona and adapt it to the emo movement that was going on in Europe —something I would never be able to get away with in Bumfuck, Alabama. Germany was the perfect place for me to develop as an artist and overall angst-filled weirdo who enjoyed the benefits of a legal drinking age of 15. As I moved up the social ladder, it was about time for Uncle Sam to knock me down a few pegs as we were once again reassigned. This time to the land that time forgot, Louisiana, where they never saw a Black person, much less a kid who dressed all in black, wore black mascara, and tied it all together with jet-black hair. Boy, that was a fun senior year…

This lifestyle was in no way a handicap. It allowed me to live a full, fast life and made me enjoy the more interesting questions of, "So, where else have you been?" and "What did you do there?" It wasn't until my stateside, sedentary mid-forties that my life completely collapsed, and my momentum crashed into me on the sidelines of my journey. I guess I just forgot to learn how to slow down, and all I saw was the wreckage of what I was becoming and the lack of humility that came from my momentum.

When you have a mental breakdown, your life stops abruptly, and the items that you were carrying—like work, family, stress, and doubts—all come smashing forward with a powerful force that you witness in slow motion, but it's still too fast to stop.

That same inertia that kept me rolling, feeling the wind in my hair and seeing the traffic piled up behind me, was also responsible for the pile-up of years of neglect, the wrong turns, and the bad exits I took to keep moving.

The force was coming from my past.

It was coming from Montana.

CHAPTER
One

THE BOY IN D5

It's been a long time since I was in Montana. I think the last time I was there, I was around 12 years old. For me, the plane trip was always the best part.

Before 9/11, airport hubs were a snapshot of America—a glance of something beyond you and the things you knew. They were places where only important people went. Captains of industry and businessmen shuffled about, each one holding briefcases and Styrofoam cups—disappearing into terminals and blending into the awful carpet with their shiny, pinstripe suits.

Heavy box television sets strained on their wall mounts as passengers looked up to see the status of their flights. And the women… my God, the WOMEN.

For a latchkey kid with access to antiquated Playboys and fuzzy cable channels, the stewardesses were Amazonian goddesses of the sky—infallible creatures whose sole purpose was to assist men with whatever they needed.

Thirsty? Here's a drink. Sleepy? Here's a pillow.

Aww, you're flying all by yourself, little boy? You are ADORABLE!

Whenever I was flying, there was always a stewardess (or flight attendant, as we say now) who was assigned to me. I used to think that they did it because I was so cute and charming, but now I realize that they probably had to draw straws in the back to see who was going to escort the goofy kid in D5.

"Damn, I'll tell you what, Karen—if you take D5, I'll take H2."

"Isn't H2 the fat, sweaty guy that grabs asses and calls us sweet stuff?… fuck it, I'll take D5."

Whatever the reason was, the stewardesses were always so nice to me. And they smelled so good. Even though the cabin was filled with different blends of smoke and sweat, they never lost the faint smell of Dial soap and oatmeal cookies.

A typical scenario was a parent dropping me off at the gate and in the trusting (and soft) hands of a stewardess. From there, I was put in my seat, which was usually a window seat so I could see how long it took for the cars and buildings to look like a Matchbox play set. As the businessmen loaded in, bumped their briefcases, and began the battle of armrest superiority, I was eagerly awaiting the coveted invitation to go beyond business class; beyond first class; beyond the galley and pressurized port-a-potties—I was going to the cockpit to hobnob with the pilot and trade war stories about our times in the air. If I smiled wide enough and charmed my way past my stupid cowlick and my awkward gait, I would get my wings!

I collected plastic airline wings like a WWII vet collected medals and Nazi memorabilia. I wore them with pride as I strolled back to my seat, passing all of the commoners and their miserable lives. Sure, they had important places to go, but I was one of the guys who would help get them there. If the plane caught on fire and the pilot and co-pilot were incapacitated, I was basically next in line. There would be no ass-grabbing on my watch, H2! Treat my girls with respect!

Back in D5, watching us taxi out and hearing my pal, Captain Dan, talking about the route and time and weather conditions over Colorado, I couldn't help feeling a mix of fear and pride.

I love traveling, and I think that bug bit with all of the trips I took as an only child of divorced parents. While other kids spent their summers visiting those same pools, playing the same games with the same friends, I was a man of adventure and worldly travel. Sure, they had the stability of two loving parents, but did they have official Delta pilot wings presented by the prestigious Captain Dan?

I think not.

That feeling you get as the nose ascends toward the sky and your stomach clutches onto your ribs and melts back toward your spine like Jello is the feeling I got when I arrived in Montana. No matter how far I flew, how many stewardesses sat with me and smiled, or how much manly secondhand smoke I consumed in the cabin of Delta Flight 1490, I was still the boy in D5.

The last memory I have of traveling to Montana is positive. I remember wanting to look older than I was, so I wore a wool suit—the only suit I had. Sure, it was summer, and I was sweating, but that's what men do. Even my perception of adulthood at 12 was spot on. Adults are stuffy, uncomfortable, and just fucking dorky.

To improve my vision of unaccompanied minor non grata, I hollowed out an old backgammon briefcase to hold all of my essential business travel necessities: an old sketchbook, pencils, and *Tales of Ramona Quimby*.

That's all I remember.

I have no idea how long I stayed, what I did, or when I returned. I can remember the smell of leather and the sensation of ears popping at 20,000 feet, but for the life of me, I can't remember the trip. Thinking back now, I can't recall most of the trips—just the journey. Every other holiday, spent with family, is overlapped with peanuts and pretzels with strangers. Long walks with loved ones are just riding an escalator up and down—killing time before the next layover. A warm, loving embrace is a low-skirt, leggy airline employee telling me that the bumps and shifts are all normal and to try and relax.

Before we had screens that fit in our pockets and ways of taking up time, we spent a lot of time with our thoughts. You know, those blips that cross our mind that we tend to distract ourselves from if they hurt and focus on if they tickle. The problem I have with thoughts is that I can't trust them.

To me, Montana has always represented the great unknown, and facing that after all these years is frightening and inevitable. It's a state and state of mind that I have purposely stayed away from for over 40 years, and now that the secrets of my past are affecting the realities of my present, I find myself at a great junction in my life. I can stay the course, hope for the best, and continue on the lost road I'm on, or return to the place where it all began and try to make sense of how I got on this path in the first place.

CHAPTER

Two

FIRST STEPS

It's May 12, 2020, now, and I just booked my flight to Montana for the first week in July. If this was any other trip, my wife, Jennifer, would be furious at me for leaving her alone with our three children. But, technically, this is all her fault.

For years, she has been wanting me to take this opportunity, and for years, I've made excuses and other plans. "You're not getting any younger, you know." "Don't you have anything you want to say to him?" "It doesn't sound good… if you're going to go, you better do it fast." Behind my wife's calm blue eyes, I can see her heart and mind struggle between what she knows is right and what she feels is right.

Whatever I can say about Jenny has been said in romantic radio ballads and French poetry. She is a marvelous woman and is exactly the person I always needed in my life—especially now. Jenny is that person you take with you to keep you out of trouble, and when they reel you in from making monstrous mistakes, you get pissy. A few hours or days will pass, and better judgment prevails, and you find yourself apologizing and thanking them for not letting you put your balls in an air fryer.

We have been married for almost 15 years, and she probably knows more about my father than I do. She's tenacious and caring—two conflicting attributes that would have made a great private investigator or public defender. Her late-night researching by the glow of her iPhone, taking notes and making scribbled family trees, has been part of her plan to have everything laid out and ready. She's a go-getter and uses her brains and charm (and sometimes cleavage to get out of a speeding ticket) to achieve her high goals, and I find myself forever out of breath trying to keep up.

So, when my father got sick for the last time, she knew I had to go but felt that I had to run this race on my own. I want to impress her, and that's why, for now, I'm not putting up much of a fight. I know deep down she is right, as usual, and in the well deep inside of me that debates right and wrong is telling me that I will go to Montana.

Eventually.

Jenny knows my father is dying, and however slowly my father's cancer is killing him, I am determined to go slower. If you could dissect my procrastination, spin it through a very slow centrifuge, and market it through Merck, you would have an antibody of cancer-slowing sludge. I watched my father's diagnosis leak like a slow spill of coffee creeping to the edge of some important papers. I knew that eventually I would have to get to it, but I didn't have the time or a paper towel nearby.

Deep in my guilt-plagued gut, I knew I would never see him again. It's hard to say goodbye when we never really said hello.

I told Parker, our oldest and only boy, that he will be the man of the house, and he assumes that he will be grilling ramen noodles and cleaning the pool. It's funny how you are perceived by the ones with the rawest perception. I have been thinking the most about our relationship lately and the roles that a father plays in a young man's life. Whenever I mess up (and it's honestly been a lot lately), Jenny reminds me that I'm the only male role model in his life, and I get depressed.

He's going to have enough to worry about in this brave new world. We had teeter-totters, and they now have TikToks. The relationship I build with him and the things I teach him are not just going to be in his memories; they will be accessible anytime on any digital device. I just want there to be a few rainbows when he's searching through his cloud.

Normally, I hate when people say "Old Soul," especially when they are referring to themselves. It's a weird and brazen attempt to make them feel as if they are more and can transcend some made-up plane that you can maybe reach in a few more lifetimes. Now, if someone says that you are an Old Soul, that is completely different.

Our middle child, Gwen, is the existential embodiment of a love that's been around for a long time. She's kind in a way that I've never seen, and she walks around asking everyone deep questions and telling them that she is almost 6. Technically, she won't be 6 until October, but she reminds us daily that she will be 6. I have to admire that determination and openness, but I don't understand how a child that has everything handed to her would ever want to leave a plush lifestyle.

She must see the shit that we do throughout the day—the constant washing and folding of clothes, the never-ending trips to Target, the bitterness we start to develop, and the way our bodies are starting to droop and show signs of slowing down. Who would want that? An Old Soul, I guess.

McKenzie, or Duck, as we call her, is three and views my trek as an opportunity to snag a sweet "Rainbow Buffalo" from the faraway kingdom of Montana. I explain to her about airplanes and flying, and she looks at me with a stare full of wonder and questions. This is a child I can identify with—staring at the nighttime sky, looking for planes and dreaming about mythical bison.

It's probably not nice to say that a child is a mistake unless you're a Baldwin, but Duck wasn't planned, and when Jenny had her at 41, it almost broke her. Our third, and largest, child led Jenny down her own path of physical and mental demise, only to come out stronger a year later.

I have two other children, both with my ex-wife. My first child, Brogan, is an adult now and doing adult things. It's interesting and special to see her navigate the world and make decisions that you are sure are wrong but turn out to be remarkable. She's headstrong and smart and uses her determination to open doors so a man doesn't have to. She is everything I joke about but would really want to be.

My second child, Hailey, starts college this fall. She lived with her mother most of her life, so our interactions and relationship are much like those of military brats. We get our hugs and laughs at Christmas, our deep conversations every other summer, and our sporadic "I have good/bad news" calls throughout. She is a remarkable artist and a loyal daughter. I can tell when she tells me something, it's true, and I see most of me in her.

I think a lot about my family before I take my next steps. I want to be sure that this trip is going to be fruitful and bear some calm in my soul. I hope that I get the answers that open me up to be a better husband, father, and person.

Fuck me, I just got the confirmation email from Delta. I'm booked. I guess I'm going.

It's odd. All of these years of pushing this aside and the month of running and ducking, I don't feel dread or panic. I don't feel the familiar response of pushing it to the side. He's gone, so I'm going. I feel relieved that he's not there and gratitude for the opportunity that I beat the clock. I feel excited to pick up relationships I've made with some of this family and make new ones. It's a feeling of opening a Christmas present and a first kiss.

But most of all, I feel thankful for my wife, who saw my pain and identified my struggle. I am thankful to be with someone who must have felt sad and faltering as her husband needed more help than she could give. I am thankful that she encouraged me to see another woman.

CHAPTER
Three

THE OTHER WOMAN

Way back when, I had the unique opportunity to be in a three-way. It was unplanned and developed innocently at an Applebee's over fried mozzarella sticks and pints of Yuengling. Not quite the sexy setting from a trashy romance novel, but hey, it wasn't a Sizzler either.

A casual female acquaintance wanted me to set up a date between her and a friend from my work that she had noticed and admired. After a lot of drinking, flirtatious banter, and closing down the bar, we headed to her place, which was within walking distance, to drink more and sober up by morning. Things took a dramatic shift when she excused herself and came back to the living room naked, holding a large, black, veiny dildo.

No pressure.

Nothing sobers you up more than looking over the cliff of inhibition and seeing the vastness of your own insecurities. However, I was a guest and didn't want to be rude, so I decided to at least follow them into the bedroom to ponder my options comfortably on a floral-pattern duvet cover.

As we all lay in bed, I knew this wasn't going to work. The logistics of what was going to go where and who was going to do what became so overwhelming that I faked falling asleep and turned my back toward the whole event. I lay there, eyes wide and mouth agape, "snoring" as loudly as I could to block out the sounds of giggling and deep breathing. It wasn't until I felt something hard and wet against my shoulder that I jumped up and shouted, "Well, I'm out!" I spent the remainder of that long evening with my eyes shut and my hands over my ears on her couch.

The next morning, I woke up to the smell of coffee and relief as the two navigated the awkwardness of the night before. Not being the third wheel—or kickstand—made me impervious to the strange banter as we all went our separate ways. The events of the night before seemed to be kept there, and needless to say, I didn't spend much time with them after that—or ever eat at an Applebee's again.

Even my ID knows I'm a disaster at mitigating even the most profound and intimate of settings. Couple that with a high degree of codependency, and you have a man who can adapt to most social situations but really is meant to be monogamous. Maybe there was a time long ago, before I drove a minivan and wore khakis, that I may have been able to pull it off, but now, as I struggle to trim nose, ear, and back hair and Google foods that increase testosterone, I can't imagine a more stressful situation.

Until I started therapy.

When a woman recommends something, it's not really a choice. It's a trick to see if you're open to an experience, and that reaction will gauge the effort you intend to put forth. For example, when a wife recommends you eat a salad, that means get off your ass and take a walk, you fat fuck.

So, when my therapist wife "recommended" I go to therapy, it brought me back to that night on the couch. I felt like an active observer who was just a vessel for a story and not actually an active participant. I was being led to an experience that I wasn't prepared for, but I was too incapacitated to find a better way back.

I thought that my waning depression and anxiety were just a precursor of midlife and maybe some repressed stuff that I was bottling up. Maybe there is a molestation somewhere in there for good measure. I was a child of the '80s, and being inappropriately fondled by a trusting adult was almost a rite of passage.

As men my age tend to do, I oppressed the feelings I was having and masked them with humor, silence, and the occasional explicit-filled monologue as to why baristas feel the need to be edgy. You're making a cappuccino, for fuck's sake—stop changing your pronouns.

It's hard for men to be vulnerable, especially to women. Historically and genetically, we are supposed to hunt the food, kill the big animal, take the occasional beating, do the perpetual screwing, and repeat.

People my age are the last of a defined dichotomy. For good or bad, we are the product of a product of a product. All of our complex morals, judgments, and core thinking are just Xerox copies of what came before. They lose their sharpness and definition as they keep going, until the point of being a cloud of jumbled symbols. I think that my copy was at the point of getting jammed in the machine.

Was it time to change the ink, reset the print heads, or just put it out of its misery? For me, therapy resembled the technician your company calls to take a look. Are they worth the time and money, or are you just going to keep kicking the damn thing until it breaks?

I started my therapy a year ago, right before the COVID pandemic of 2020. I was confident that I had hit the low. Little did I know that *my* low was deep, deep down in the mud and grit. Past the snails and worms and the heat of the sun. We're talking Mole Men low.

As I sat in the waiting room, I grew annoyed. The clock read 9:10.

My appointment was at 9:00, and I sat alone on a stiff IKEA chair, surrounded by wood paneling and copies of *Good Housekeeping* with the address labels cut out.

9:11 a.m.

I do the loud sigh so the receptionist hears me. I shuffle my feet and even stand up to stretch—a universal sign that too much blood has gone to my ass on account of me sitting here 10 EXTRA MINUTES!

Clearly, she knows I'm here and seems unflustered and disengaged as she sips from her mug that says, "Sunshine is the best medicine."

"How the fuck did I get here?" I ask myself.

"Is it weird if I just leave?"

"Do I make a scene as I storm off like a dollar-store version of Matt Damon in *Good Will Hunting*?"

"Oh, I know… I can say, 'You know what? Being on time and considerate of other people's time is the best medicine!' Fucking genius!"

Christ, this must be a common thing in therapy. Maybe it gives them some psychological upper hand by having us stand by. Maybe they know that you can't really ask for a manager because, technically, they are working for you—so you're the manager! What am I going to do, talk to myself? If I talk to myself, then I really have problems, and this generalized anxiety stuff can take a back seat.

Calm down. Breathe.

Speaking of back seats, I can't stop thinking about my therapist driving in her car, listening to an a cappella, acoustic version of an underground Dave Matthews recording that only millennial hipsters know about. I bet she even has one of those bumper stickers that says "Coexist" in every Eastern religion symbol that ever—

"Holy shit, is that her car?" I say to myself as I see a salt-covered dark Honda pulling in. I squint to read what's right above the right taillight.

Bernie 2020. Close enough.

Nicole was exactly how I imagined her before I even knew I needed therapy—an artsy woman in her late 30s with a big red smile and comforting presence, and despite her tardiness, I accepted the fact that her education, job, and title of LCPC granted her some carte blanche. She wiped her feet at the worn doormat, said good morning to the receptionist, and fumbled for her keys in her oversized bag.

She was recommended to me by my wife's friend in a late-night, vague Facebook post to a local mom group. Jenny asked, "Does anyone know a good therapist that focuses on men's issues?" Now, everyone knows when you say "friend," it's you or someone close to you. Within minutes, most of her friends recommended a good erectile dysfunction doctor, but one of her friends direct-messaged her that she knew of a great therapist who would be perfect for me. I couldn't shake the feeling that everyone in our circle of virtual friends and modest family now considered the possibility that I had some form of ED problems or some kind of addiction.

"You must be Garth?" Nicole said as her keys jingled. "I'll be right with you."

Nicole politely guided me to a dimly lit grey couch, and I had flashbacks of the three-way—but instead of the random spontaneity of two sexual psychopaths, this was a deeper probe between a woman who wanted me to get help and the professional who maybe could help. I'm still not sure which one was worse.

The room began to close in on me, and I felt the pressure of disclosing how I was truly feeling and the anxiety of what was to come. If every journey starts with a first step, I was about to plunge headfirst into a world of deconstructing the last four decades and reliving things I either didn't know or couldn't trust, and I was already exhausted.

For months, my wife was trying to get me to commit to some form of therapy, and I was reluctant. Truthfully, I never considered the possibility that therapy could actually help. It was more of a bandage—like alcohol or denial—that was meant to pacify my loved ones and let me make it through another few weeks before the weight of stuffing it all in crushed me. It was a fantasy of a distraction that required insights and talking. Lots of talking. In a way, therapy was like drinking at a bar, and I was prepared to receive the same advice and empathy that I would get from a drunken stranger on a Saturday night.

Nicole and I proceeded to start the intake, and it was obvious to me that this was going to be the easy part of our first meeting—and I was screwed.

"Father's medical history?"

"I have no idea."

"Mother's medical history?"

"She doesn't talk about it."

"What brings you to therapy?"

"Guilt."

I don't know if she thought I was being a dick. I imagine schizophrenics hear and divulge more, and bipolar people tell her twice as much. It wasn't my intention to be so closed off so fast. I imagined that would come later, when she asked me about my lack of apathy and general displeasure for my life. After an awkward 30 minutes of filling out an empty intake on my family history, it was time to move on to the root cause of fixing me completely in the remaining 30 minutes.

"So, really, tell me what's going on?" my therapist Nicole said casually as I took a seat on a plush green chair. I looked around and saw the contrast of colorful paintings and muted hues of tissue boxes spread strategically along the armchairs. I took a deep breath and remembered the pain I was causing myself and my family. I saw the look in my kids' eyes as I lay on a cold grey couch, dissociated and empty. I heard the desperation in my wife's voice, pleading with me to get help.

And then I shared my first true feeling.

"To be honest, I'm not quite sure… I guess I just feel… lost."

I think that was the first time I said it. Out loud, anyway.

"Why…?"

CHAPTER

Four

RULES

RULE: MEN DON'T ASK FOR DIRECTIONS/HELP

It goes without saying that a civilized and modern society can only achieve social and economic bliss by conforming to certain standards that benefit the greater good. Rules are set in place by unanimous, faceless committees over long periods of time, to the point that we just widely accept them as a way of life. If you challenge these norms, there are usually consequences. The broad rule structures all boil down to surrendering to the ideology of right and wrong.

What I didn't know at the time—and what I was soon to learn—would be the greatest revelation to my psyche and overall mental health. My rule structure was so deeply ingrained that even bending them caused panic and anxiety.

I sat staring at a paisley painting of an elephant that was adjacent to the wooden bookcase of DSMs, self-help guides, and Milton Bradley games. Then I looked at the Kleenex, clumped over and void of color or any distinguishable shape or weight.

My eyes shifted back and forth as I fought to decide what direction this journey would ultimately be taking me. In the middle was Nicole, who sat across from me on a couch sipping what I can only imagine was some kind of green, minty tea that you can only get from a store that sells healing crystals and chimes glistening with loosely translated Hindu sayings.

"Describe what you mean by lost?" she asked.

"I guess I just don't feel like I'm where I need to be or doing what I want to be doing."

"What do you want to be doing?"

"I dunno," I said, "anything that I want to. Anything besides watching kids, suffering from rejected proposals, and the overall repetitive melancholy people feel day after day."

"That's a pretty vague answer. Can you elaborate?"

"Sure..."

RULE: IT'S NOT SUPPOSED TO BE LIKE THIS

I became a father for the first time at the age of 25, fresh out of a six-year enlistment in the Army, to a woman I had been married to since I was 18.

"Too young?" Probably. "That's crazy!" Not really.

I was a military brat from around age nine, when my stepfather, Karl Gerhart, or "Pops," as I called him, dropped his rolling stone and traded in his cemented boots and marginal paycheck to enlist in the U.S. Army. For the next nine years, I would be towed around from state to state and country to country, taking in the vast culture of Europe and being humbled by the sophisticated ways Louisianians sucked crawfish shit out of their necks at a place called Jessie's Night Heat.

Brats are highly adaptable and, depending on the number of deployments, long for some stability.

When I arrived in Kaiserslautern, Germany, as a pimple-faced, suspender-wearing art kid, I met my ex. In retrospect, and with years of wisdom behind me, I realize that I need to be in a relationship. So when a much more direct member of the fairer sex pursued me, I took that infectious advancement as love. We finished high school, spent a few months pursuing higher education, and decided to rejoin the only way of living we knew. We both joined the Army.

After six years of enlistment, I had called it quits. I wanted to find my purpose beyond marching and late-night details. I wanted to be an artist. Whatever that means. So I left. She stayed, and we both should have known that was a prolific, symbolic warning of things to come.

Twelve years, three deployments, and two kids later, we were different people moving at different speeds and yet still crashing into each other. So we split the kids, holidays, and assets and moved on to our respective next chapters.

So when I was in my 30s, I had vigor and ambition. I wasn't tailing and curtailing someone else's career and ambitions. I was free to succeed or fail on my own.

I spent the remainder of our session talking about how life wasn't fair and how starting a new family with a new mortgage and new schools was making me angry. I expressed that not having an immediate family around to help and being at the will of playdates, doctor visits, and late-night shit-diaper patrol was making me feel like I was drowning.

"I thought my life was going to be easier in my 40s," I admitted. "I'm on the back nine of life, and this is the point where I am supposed to relax, look over my accomplishments, settle in, and start a nice coast downward. I'm supposed to be Conan at the end of *Conan*, where he sits on his throne, content in his victories and reminiscing about what's good in life."

Nicole wrote something in her notebook that took a lot longer than I think it should have.

What is she writing? Probably, *NOTE TO SELF: WATCH CONAN.*

Then she looked up from her notebook and peered at me above the heavy, dark frames of her glasses and said the three most important words I would use to move forward.

"Who said so?" she responded, as stoic and casually as someone asking for the time.

"Um…" I was so lost and confused.

My own unwritten, unbreakable rules that had guided my decisions and motivated my actions were unwound with three simple words. My mind tried to bend the phrasing and interpret the question as rhetorical. I sat still and sank lower as I searched my mental database for a proverb or professor that I could reference, a friend or colleague that may have slipped a shot of wisdom into my psyche after a night of drinking, or even a blurb I read from my wife's self-help magazines.

Nada.

"I said so."

"Well, who are you?"

RULE: DON'T ANSWER A QUESTION WITH A QUESTION

Goddamn psychotherapy has been so overdone to the point of being mocked. Fifty years since Freud thought "motherfucker" was a thesis and not an insult. When I used to berate and belittle my male friends who were having a rough time, I would pretend to put on glasses, pull out a notepad, touch the tip of my imaginary pen to my tongue, and say, "How does that make you feel?" This tactic is the adult version of "You gonna cry to mommy?"

In male-speak, answering a question with a question shows uncertainty and weakness, so I could feel my defenses rising. I came to therapy for answers, just like I would go to take my car in for service. When you drop off your car because it sputters and smokes every time you stop at a stop sign, and the professional in the shop says, "Ya got me, Buddy… what do *you* think?" it doesn't inspire much confidence.

I sat there like an idiot feeling gypped—not because of the question to the question, but because I was almost out of time. I looked at the clock and groaned inside as the minute hand crept to the 12. There is nothing more frightening than being left with uncertainty.

"Who am I?" I thought. Not just at that moment, but who was I, really? Was I a father? Was I a son? A husband? A friend? Was the sum of my life valued by how much money I made, or by the impressions and connections I made along the way?

Therapy is a lot like traveling. You have to have a reason to go, some direction, and be open to the possibilities that the journey can take you on. Without having a goal, direction, and purpose, you are just wandering. Wandering through your problems and your past will lead you to be more lost than when you started.

As we become older and cursed by life's little worries, our travels seem to be less about living a purposeful life and more about finding happiness and contentment. A good therapist is like a travel agent.

Sure, you're about to take the trip alone, but you may miss out on better seats and extra little bags of pretzels.

Like a long trip, the first leg was soon over, and I was left questioning where to pick up my bags. There was a small tear that was opened, and as I walked to my car on that cold January morning, that tear became a hole that wasn't leaking but was eager to be filled.

I wanted more.

RULE: WE'RE ALL GOING TO FUCKING DIE

The weeks passed, and my next appointment became smack dab in the fever of the COVID pandemic. Suddenly, my issues seemed petty amid a strain of super flu that we thought would fill your lungs with sharp burrs and cause you to choke on your own bile. Just as I was taking preemptive action to alleviate stress, worry, and doubt from my psyche, I now had to shift into caveman survival mode because we were all going to die because we touched a doorknob without wearing a hazmat suit.

Probably not since World War II or the Trump inauguration was society so certain that we were headed for a global disaster.

Information was limited, and each "specialist" and political operative had their own predictions and solutions. Even now, as the world opens and returns to normal, there is no clear consensus as we move forward like lemmings jumping off a cliff or soldiers going to battle. But, hey, we are sure that our side is right, and the other side are all idiots.

The difference in thinking, social and political variants, and religious vs. scientific dilemmas tend to affect people like me who are most content in dichotomous situations that make us choose a side. Once someone who has clear rules and boundaries is forced into a situation that can have life-or-death consequences, our rules become more rigid and abstract.

I recall a few days before our state of Maryland was going to be shut down to "slow the curve." Our federal and local governments set in place their own set of rules that protected the country's wellness as a whole by locking up and bearing down.

RULE: DON'T TRUST THE GOVERNMENT

When my local government can't fix the pothole outside my house or tear down a statue because they once rode a horse who was bred by a man whose grandfather ate at a southern mansion that once housed a slave, I tend to try and find my own solution. I find it hard to believe that our country's saviors are going to be the ones who can beat a global pandemic in two weeks when they have been fighting the same wars for decades. I guess years of being a latchkey kid gave me perspective early on about how to take care of myself when mommy and daddy were too busy.

Preparedness is thinking five steps forward and seeing things play out in the worst possible way. I imagined a world shut down for weeks, months, and years. I played out scenarios of a population where food trucks couldn't make it to grocery stores because the drivers were all sick or dead. I imagined Lord Humungous speaking gruffly to a collective outpost of survivors to "leave the hot dogs and shit paper and go." I collaborated with like-minded individuals in sketchy Facebook groups about which ammo stores sold the most rounds and what frequency we would all use to link up when society fell.

667.9 MHZ FYI.

It was clear that I had a problem with rules, but not in the traditional, rebellious sense. I didn't want to break them; I wanted everyone to respect and follow them. I didn't want the world on my terms; I wanted it on even terms.

The elusiveness of emotional stability and my fragile sense of fairness became more apparent the more I spoke to Nicole. One of the most wonderful parts of therapy is the selfish sabbatical you can take with a person who doesn't depend on you. It's an hour of release and unstructured dialogue that doesn't need a response or an opinion.

After all, it's easier to reflect on a green velour couch with a trained professional than shouting alone from a self-made soapbox. In the wake of my hour of honesty, I finally began to see the root of my problem. Life wasn't playing fair to my rules.

"So, when should we set up your next appointment to discuss how we can maybe whittle down some of these false narratives you've created?" Nicole said with a smile as she closed my file.

"Wait… there's more?"

"Oh God, yes. How does next week sound?"

CHAPTER

Five

DRUGS V. MEDICINE

Sorting out my past and challenging my rule structure wasn't going to be easy. It was going to be a painful exploration into my subconscious, and it was going to get messy. It was going to take more than compassion from my wife, understanding from my family, and countless therapy sessions. It was going to take drugs. Lots of drugs.

When I was officially diagnosed with depression and ADHD, I ran the gauntlet of self-help articles and weekly therapy visits with Nicole. I pushed hard to try and avoid taking any drugs. Not only did I personally have the worst experience with medication, I had a stigma that taking drugs —any drugs, albeit Tylenol—was for losers.

Since my dive into utter despair, I have battled over the nomenclature and effectiveness of pharmaceuticals. Being an '80s-era brat and having adverse reactions to any form of legal or illegal medication, I have always referred to them as "drugs," and as Mr. T and Nancy Reagan always told us…

RULE: DRUGS ARE BAD

My wife's occupation and history with said experiences has precluded her from referring to it as "medicine." And so, the battle of drugs versus medicine ignites in the Gerhart household.

My first illegal substance was a cigarette. It was technically illegal because I was only six years old, and even for the '80s, that was a bit extreme. I was wandering around with a group of older kids, and one had a pack of Lucky Strikes he stole from his mother. Since most mothers smoked at the time, we all assumed it was copacetic as we each took our first long drag. We knew immediately that smoking was bad as we hacked and coughed in the dusty pit we hid in. Somehow, I felt guilt over the nausea and tried to cover my deed from my mother by not speaking the whole night. I was certain that she would smell the smoke on my breath. I mimed my way through dinner, and somewhere between NBC primetime and bedtime, I oversold it and came clean. My punishment was a week without *Battlestar Galactica*; a small price to pay for stepping into adulthood.

My later experiences with drugs were just as bad and shameful. I never understood why most of my friends raved about pot. Maybe since it was always classified as a "gateway drug," I was immune to their peer pressure. Growing up traveling the world, I think it was more acceptable and cosmopolitan to dabble in recreational drugs, but I somehow knew that gateway drugs would have the potential to open a floodgate.

Not that I'm against all sin, mind you. Germany, for example, was a haven for debauchery—so much so that my high school was a block away from 40 Mark Strasse. Calculating inflation and taxes, 40 marks was about 20 dollars and would get you whatever you wanted from a prostitute on that road. The only catch, besides VD, was you had to do your business in a small, compact car, and it was done with an experienced woman with an average age of 60. I'm all for women empowerment and equal pay, but banging a grandma for 20 dollars in a Geo Metro seemed cheap in every sense. But if the local government deemed it acceptable, then who was I to question 100 years of sound German politics?

The one "drug" that was always accessible, never gross, and completely legal was alcohol. I realized that if you take away the threat of incarceration, make it taste good, and give you a buzz, I was in. The potency and quantity of German spirits and Hefeweizen made me quite the contender when I eventually moved back stateside. As I slayed many southern gentlemen under the table of the rotgut bars of Louisiana in my senior year, I tried another type of drug.

If you are a creative or paranoid person by nature, I DO NOT recommend hallucinogens. After a night of innocent senior week drinking in the Cajun country of Leesville, Louisiana, a few of my native friends took me up to Alligator Lake to try shrooms. My best friend, Chris, and I were both military brats and the only ones who were out of place in a dark cow pasture on a hot summer night. Drunk on 40 ounces of Old Milwaukee and sober on the idea of being an adult, we followed our peers to fresh piles of manure, enlistment, and fear. As Chris swallowed a few mushrooms, I observed him before I would try. He played out on the hood of my car and looked up at the stars, smiling. After a few minutes, he was delighted when his first trip allowed him to lasso the moon and pull it down to him like some space cadet George Bailey. Eager to experience this wonderful life, I filled my mouth with shitty fungi and sprawled next to my friend, eager for my turn at Nirvana.

"Meow," called a cat somewhere in the darkness. "MEOW!" the cat bellowed again in a slow, demonic tone.

I looked over at Chris to see if he heard the caterwaul, and he was locked in the contentment and safety of the golden moon. I peered down by the hood of my old Ford and saw a black cat looking at me. It whispered one more time, "meow," as it slowly turned inside out like a wet pant leg stuck on a foot. The muscles and tendons dripped and glistened against the light of Chris's moon, and it hobbled toward me, screaming MEOW with each bloody step.

I was frozen in fear and slid off my car into a thicket of weeds. The cat kept crawling toward me—"MEOW, MEOW, MEOW"—and the weeds grew and slithered around me. I looked up at Chris, who was now part of the sky, his hands swirling nebulas and his eyes bright pockets of gas. He evaporated into glitter dust, and I felt abandoned.

I don't remember what happened after that. I remember waking up around all of the participants in that same field that was smaller and less menacing than the night before. From that day forward, I never tried hallucinogens again... or liked cats.

I still enjoyed the occasional cigarette and enjoyed drinking every day with my friends. Drinking laws were practical.

A few years ago, I thought I would try pot again. Since it was legal in most states and there had been countless sitcoms about recreational drug use, I figured it was safe to give it another go. I have always had bad migraines and started to feel general anxiety about the state of my life. I had a few friends who applied for and were accepted for medicinal marijuana. I talked to my doctor, and he gave me the impression that I could be a candidate for this plan as well. The whole thing still seemed shady, and instead of his common doctorate ramblings, he communicated with nods and raised eyebrows.

Before going through with the legal bureaucracy of actually applying for my pot license, I reached out to a friend who had one for treating his anxiety. He let me sample the state's wares and assured me that this was chemically engineered to amplify the euphoria and eliminate the paranoia. My wife and I tucked in the children, went on the back deck, and I took three giant hits under her watchful and sober eye. I spent the rest of the evening on the bathroom floor with my fingers forcing my eyes to stay wide, convinced that if I were to blink, I would die.

RULE: AGAIN, DRUGS ARE BAD

I convinced myself that I would do anything I could to come back to my former state for Jenny's sake. Her worry and focus on me over the last few months made me feel worse, and I saw myself less as a partner and more as another child. It was the first time I can remember that I completely and voluntarily thrust my trust into a single person.

Not only did Jenny have the professional qualifications to help me, but she also had the history and understanding to nurture me through my recovery.

Through her contacts and investigations, she came across a psychiatrist that she thought would be a good fit. There was a certain sense of security I felt with our first virtual meeting as she greeted me with a thick European accent and called me "Mr. Garth."

Little did I know that Dr. Fowler was a rare find in the Coo-Coo Community. Not only was she thorough with her assessment, including an embarrassing discussion about the frequency and stamina of my boners, but she seemed extremely caring and concerned.

Still, as I sat in our virtual psychiatry sessions, I couldn't help but feel ashamed and vulnerable. As Dr. Fowler was going over the brands of medication that I would be volunteering to go on for the rest of my life, I felt helpless. Like a diabetic or asthmatic, I would be dependent on a pill to basically stay alive, and trusting something so small and synthetic was scary—especially with my history and skepticism about "drugs."

After an hour of planning my regimen with Dr. Fowler, I was put on my first psychiatrically prescribed controlled substance. Escitalopram, or Lexapro, was my first venture into chemically treating my mental health, and even at the lowest dose, of course, there were side effects.

I found solace and humility in imagining myself in one of those antidepressant commercials you see sandwiched between the new Toyota Tundra ad and the incredible first look at the new Disney/Pixar movie. I thought of myself walking outside through a strapless window door with raw steaks on my plate as all of my perfect friends and family played in the perfect grass outside my perfect backyard. I saw myself smiling as I cooked the 100% Angus grass-fed ribeye, hearing the voiceover talk about what Lexapro can do for you. Then the sky gets dark as the voiceover turns serious and tells you about what could go wrong. My friends and family start slowly laughing at me as I look down at my steak to see that I am grilling Buddy, my perfect golden retriever. My head spins, and I collapse in exhaustion over the burning coals and charred remains of the family dog. I catch fire, and my loved ones gather around to roast marshmallows over my flaming flannel shirt and combustible khakis.

A week or so after my steady stream of the SSRI, I wasn't on fire and my dogs remained raw and unseasoned, but I was exhausted—like, really exhausted. Unlike that depressed tired where you feel nothing and don't want to be anywhere, I wanted to be present, and I was feeling more fulfilled than I had been in a long time. This exhaustion was followed by nausea that I was told would pass in a few days. If I wasn't falling asleep at bizarre times, I was hovered over the toilet. I felt like a kid with crutches watching his friends play on the jungle gym.

Sure, I was present, but boy did I want to swing!

If you've never been prescribed a mood stabilizer from a trusted clinical professional, I recommend you approach it with the same reverence as you approach losing your virginity. The first time is awkward, and you're in awe of how you even got to this point. The more you "do it," the more you get used to the spike in serotonin and realize that you may eventually hit that sweet spot.

Dosing to get the exact right level was a test of perseverance and mental acuity. For the next several months, Dr. Fowler and I experimented with times and quantities of when and how to take the Lexapro. If I took it before noon, I would be tired at dinner. If I took it before bed, I would wake up too early. If I took too much, I would be checked out all day. If I took too little, I would be too irritable. It really was a crapshoot. I began to envy the street addicts who could figure it out on their own and get a quick fix without going through all the extra bullshit.

Nevertheless, trial and error was better than where I was at, so I proceeded slowly down the path until the good doctor told me that this particular medication might not be the right one for me and that now I would have to start the whole process over again with a new medication. Unbeknownst to me, there was a slew of medication that was basically the same thing, aside from a compound here and there.

"Well," I thought, "we're in the middle of a pandemic, and I have dick else to do but treat my body like a lab rat so I can step on a plane without having a fucking panic attack."

CHAPTER

Six

PACK TO UNPACK

RULE: IF YOU'RE NOT EARLY YOU'RE LATE

Getting ready for a trip of any kind requires me to acknowledge—and at this point, challenge—some very deeply ingrained rules. I have no idea how "normal" people don't stress about flights. Getting to the airport three hours early, triple-checking the bag weight and dimensions, and updating the flight status on the airline app is all part of the fun of modern travel. I admire people like my wife who seem to be able to just roll out of bed and have confidence that things will work out. If my tenure in the Army has taught me anything, it's that the early bird doesn't catch an ass chewing.

When I travel, I like to go light to avoid any hangups at the baggage claim. Years ago, my parents sent me to my grandfather for the summer in Tennessee, and he had a whole library of old *Playboys* in his basement. I was particularly fond of the Nancy Drew and Vanna White issues, so I figured I would discreetly pack them and reuse them back at home, where I had a fresh supply of white socks awaiting my return.

Of course, after all my trips to and from Montana, this was the bag that got lost. I felt like a pirate sneaking past colonial blockades as I yearned to find and unbury my dirty black bag full of hormonal booty. A few days later, the bag was returned, and luckily my parents were at work. I dove through the bag, shuffling through tighty-whities and *Archie Comics* to free my girls, and 40 seconds after finding them, I hid them safely in my closet.

In 2021, we don't have to worry about that. The only embarrassment I can imagine having is if I go to board, open my e-ticket, and it accidentally opens to my last browser window of "Blonde Slut gargles 56 Black Horse Cocks." At least the flight attendants will know I'm not a racist and may upgrade my seat to keep me away from children and pets.

My wife usually does the packing, mostly because I spend more time worrying about how not to look like a tourist. I remember when we went to Disneyland, I asked her, "Do you think I should pack my Batman T-shirt?"

Her lightning-fast, snarky reply: "I don't know, Garth—should any 40-year-old man wear a Batman T-shirt?"

So I'm keeping it simple. How does one even pack for a memorial in the mountains of Montana? I mean, anyone with even a passing appreciation for pop culture and irony would have to appreciate the Bruce Wayne angle of my Batman T-shirt, right? He lost his dad; I lost my dad. He grew up to be a dark, brooding man; I grew up to be a dark, brooding man.

The only real difference is that he'd be taking a private jet, while I'd be leaning forward in anticipation, waiting to hear my boarding row called.

RULE: I'M BATMAN

Batman never needed anything that he didn't have and never had anything he didn't need. He was a man of international (and sometimes cosmic) travel who knew how to pack. I'm sure some things were SOP, like packing a grappling hook and smoke bombs, but he always thought 20 steps ahead when thinking of what he may need. Everyone remembers the time when Adam West's Batman was attacked by a shark and just happened to have shark repellent in his utility belt. Do you think that was coincidence? Fuck no! Batman analyzed the data, reckoned the environment, jerked off in the Batcave to enhance his focus and calm his mind, and made the tactical assumption that there would be a shark. I wasn't anticipating any sharks on this journey, but I did come prepared with something far more general.

Amid my jeans and shoes, tucked securely between my jockeys and tattered Steinbeck, was my haul of psychiatric-prescribed Selective Serotonin Reuptake Inhibitor, or SSRIs. Like The Dark Knight, I had the insight and tools to combat any diabolical fiend that I would confront. "Oh, no! You're about to unleash 40-plus years' worth of tears and snot into the chicken salad at the wake!" Quick! Take the small white pill! "Dammit! Here comes some feelings about neglect and abandonment!" Take the large blue one!

Even with my Pablo Escobar swagger and manifest, I have zero idea how the hell this works. I know that people must bring vitamins and lifesaving medication with them, but is there a different set of rules for antidepressants? I can see an overweight man in first class, whose arteries are coated in bacon fat and mashed potatoes, suddenly clutching his chest. I can hear the pilot asking the passengers if anyone on the flight is a doctor. Then the woman next to him, who I assume is his wife but is suspiciously younger and attractive, yells, "He needs his pills!" at which point she scrambles through his carry-on bag to retrieve his heart medication. The flight attendants and first-class passengers look on as she massages the two orange pills down his throat like an old dog taking heartworm pills. She follows it up with a glass of water and a few loud slaps on his back. He coughs a few times, clears his throat, and says something hilarious to cover his embarrassment like, "Glad I decided to carry her on!" We all laugh and clap and go back to our in-flight entertainment of making uncomfortable conversations and declining the extra bag of pretzels.

Antidepressants should be given out as easily and eagerly as pretzels. I imagine at least half of the people flying are going to, or coming back from, someplace they don't want to. If half of marriages end in divorce and families split up, that's easily a quarter of the people. No one is going to states like Idaho and Kentucky unless someone old died. Funeral travel probably easily makes up another 25 percent. Right now, there are around 50 percent of people traveling that would rather be home.

"Mr. Gerhart, will there be anything else you need before takeoff?"

"No thanks, Alfred. I'm all set."

CHAPTER

Seven

LOST MARBLES

One thing I remember about my childhood visits to Montana was the horrors of fires and how quickly they can start, spread, and destroy. I remember my father wearing his Forest Service outfit and how his taupe uniform would look and smell after a day of fighting fires. As I got older and my fears of soot and ash were replaced by a general understanding of fifth-grade science, I knew that the havoc was caused by three natural elements—fuel, oxygen, and heat.

I'm pretty sure the fuel that brought me to therapy was how much I needed to confront my obsessive rule structure with Nicole. The oxygen (or lack thereof) was the medication piece that was slowly gasping between asphyxia and apnea. Now, the only element left to ignite a meltdown was the heat.

Hello, Covid!

Protecting my family, especially during a pandemic, made me more of a mess than usual. I watched Pops take care of me and my mother selflessly as he brought home meal rations from his army posts and sold his plasma weekly to save money for Christmas presents. For most men, once you have a family, the natural instinct is to protect. Your needs become secondary as you become the savior. As a man and father during the Coronavirus pandemic, I had to ensure the survival of not just me, but my wife and five kids.

Unchallenged, I think I have the normal amount of paranoia and mistrust that a middle-aged, white, suburban man would have. I walk on the other side of the street when I pass a group of teenagers; I don't stop for any red lights in downtown Baltimore between the hours of 5:00 p.m. and 6:30 a.m.; and I never… EVER… eat pizza from 7-11.

The thing about losing your mind is that you don't think you've lost your mind. Your perception becomes so askew that you rationalize irrational behavior and think that everyone else is insane. You buy ammo vests and quick-draw gun holsters while everyone else buys swimsuits and sarongs, but you think that they are selfishly unprepared. You watch everyone embrace new friendships and nurture relationships, but you view such things as commodities and plot how you will manipulate or ravage them when the lights go out forever. For someone like me, who suffers from ADHD and is prone to flights of whimsy and distraction, I was hyperaware of what was going on and filled my lackadaisical mindset with fear and paranoia. I replaced fun, open-ended projects with dire routines like checking locks and hoarding food. My basement, which was once filled with charcoal drawings and oil paintings, was becoming overrun with bottled water jugs and canned food. The things that I used to enjoy became a burden, and the only focus I had was to keep my family safe.

RULE: ALWAYS BE PREPARED

How far was I going to ensure our survival? Well, if my Amazon recent order list was any indication, I was prepared to drink water from a dirty puddle with a LifeStraw and hightail it out of town with a Rand McNally Road Atlas that I pre-plotted with back-road escape routes, because the main highways would surely be taken over by roving gangs of mole men. I even thought of how I may have to barter for rations or our lives with luxury items, so I bought $200 worth of Marlboro Lights and massive quantities of Jack Daniels (which can also be used to sterilize medical equipment and dull pain should one be shot with an arrow or bitten by a zombie).

Days were spent buying munitions and stocking up on supplies. Nights were spent patrolling the house and scouring the internet to find the "truth" about how the next few weeks were going to play out. Not only was I losing my marbles, but I was also losing sleep. I would see things dart across me that weren't there. Shapes and patterns would appear to close in on me, and I just gradually accepted it because this is the way things would be now.

I started training myself to live on 500 calories a day and two-minute ice-cold showers. I printed out manuals on what plants to eat, which to avoid, and how to skin and cook small game. I started to adapt a minimalist lifestyle—not to find joy in owning less, but to stuff everything I own into a bug-out bag.

Ironically, the ones I was trying to protect were the ones I was hurting the most.

My wife, Jenny, and I are very compatible despite being complete opposites. If Paula Abdul could find love with a dancing, animated cat, then surely I could find love with a type-A, well-educated, attractive, OCD hypochondriac.

For most of our relationship, she has been the voice of reason and has gratefully stopped me from making such bad decisions as buying land in Nova Scotia and changing careers to be a nomadic carpenter. However, when it comes to the heat of the moment and her obvious sexual attraction to men of lower stock and higher pounce, she carelessly has thrown out sound judgment and birth control and delivered three of my hellspawn.

When I moved back to Maryland to start a new life and a new job, I found that the world of dating and meeting people had gone digital, and my old ways of creepily and desperately staring at women across a bar until they felt sorry for me or called the police no longer worked. A friend who had just met someone on Myspace suggested I make a profile, and within minutes a list of local women in my area popped up. I was overwhelmed with the prospects and felt weirded out by the whole process until I saw a long-faced, smiling blonde therapist posing with a giant picture of Al Roker.

Maybe it was fate or my affinity for early-morning talk shows, but I sent her a message. That message turned into a response. That response turned into emails, and the emails turned into late-night talks and bantering about our favorite bands and our worst relationships. It would be a month of getting to know her through texts and calls before we met face-to-face, and once we met, I was done. We met at a local brewery, and I was hooked on her like the drag of the Camel Light we shared and felt as bubbly as the rim of our beer glasses.

I should have known that with all my messed-up baggage, I would be dating a therapist. I didn't know that I needed a therapist yet; I just knew I needed THAT therapist.

Being in a relationship with a mental health provider is like fucking the pool boy. They both have specialized skills that most people don't want to do because it's tedious, and when the fun is over, they are kind of expected to, well, clean the dirty spaces. The skill set that defines and rewards you carries over to every relationship. I'm somewhat of an artist, and I can't tell you how many times people want me to make business cards and draw pictures of their goofy kids.

However, the pool boy's hose and my Adobe software are not responsible for someone's mental wellness. I imagine anyone in the health field has a tricky time separating that title from their personal life.

For us, as a registered codependent couple, we share our experiences deeply and take it upon ourselves to heal the other. I am generally optimistic and spontaneous, so when my wife is down, I take it upon myself to "fix" her mood. I crack a joke or, in most cases, minimize her problems. This tactic usually results in her misreading my intention as passive and uncaring. On the other hand, she will sense my cynical, insecure, moody-artist "nothing I do will ever be good enough" vibe as an opportunity to use her training to heal my internal struggle. This causes me to feel worse about myself by not being a stronger, more secure husband to her. Even though both of our intentions are noble, we end up doing more damage. Hence, the cycle continues.

Around Election Day, at the great height of my maddening, I contacted a Canadian lawyer. My unbiased and fact-based research led me to believe that if Donald Trump won the 2020 presidential election, Antifa and other media-driven, anti-democracy groups would rise up and burn cities in protest. Also, if Joe Biden won, right-wing "patriots" would contest the victory by rising up and burning cities. Not since *Alien vs. Predator* had the stakes been so high and the risk of survival so low.

My contact in Canadian law not only made me sound like a badass, but it also put me at a great advantage to find a path to citizenship before the other fools realized our country had fallen to tyranny and my family and I were the only ones smart enough to see the destruction coming. The Canuck I made contact with was established and came highly recommended in finding quick ways toward citizenship. He and I developed a plan to use my job title as "artist" to come in on a betterment-of-society work visa. He assured me that my dick and fart jokes for *Mad Magazine* made me a prime candidate to act as an ambassador of artistic enlightenment for our northern neighbors.

Using this fail-proof and totally legal way to gain entry into Canadian soil would only cost me five grand and put me on a waiting list to enter within two years. If the Covid numbers kept steady and we could hold the country's collapse together for just a few short months, my family and I would be safe in Canada.

Since my wife grew up and works with chaos, my actions seemed somewhat odd but mostly reasonable based on my never having gone bat-shit crazy before. Immediately, I started planning to shift our assets, take the kids out of school, and buy a house in Canada.

The lawyer gave me the weekend to settle my affairs, allocate the five grand, and find suitable housing before he could start the process. In the meantime, I started to fill out the appropriate paperwork for the visas.

To my wife's credit, she had been extremely cool with my erratic behavior up to the point when I sent her a list of houses with the text, "Pick one."

RULE: WOMEN ARE STUBBORN

After a mental health check with her own therapist, my therapist wife confronted me in the dark recesses of my basement command center. Among the piles of coffee-stained paperwork, open browser screens of houses in Winnipeg, and an auto-replaying YouTube video of *"How to Live Off Drinking Your Own Urine,"* she calmly said, "Garth. Honey. Do you think you might be having a mental breakdown?"

"No, why?" I replied as I clicked "confirm" on my order of bulletproof socks and MREs.

"Well, I was talking to Jon (her therapist), and I was telling him what has been going on, and he seems concerned. He said it sounds like you are going through a mental breakdown. I immediately started to defend you, but I thought about it, and I think you may be taking things a bit too far."

It took me years to quit smoking. I always made an excuse to keep doing it, even though I knew how bad it was. Time after time, giving up and giving in, it never took until I was 45. That's almost 25 years of smoking.

I stopped this obsession immediately. Hearing the words said out loud—"mental breakdown"—brought a self-actualization that stopped me. I felt like a computer riddled with spam and viruses that just got a hard reboot. I was functioning at full capacity, my hard drive clear—born again.

RULE: SUCK IT UP AND DRIVE ON

Fuck yeah, I was cured!

Like a good, strong man, incapable of folly and void of introspection, I left it all there, unattended and unaddressed, as I moved on with the life that I knew before my breakdown.

Like everything else that made me sad, anxious, or depressed, I packed it away deep inside and decided not to face it. I was working on challenging my rules, facing my past, and my new friends Johnson and Johnson had given me the tools to fight both fronts. A mental breakdown was just going to be a distraction, so my fight-or-flight instinct kicked in, and I incorrectly chose the latter.

The human body is an amazing vessel that can withstand a shit ton of physical trauma. From the quick release of pain receptors to the slow endurance of those freak shows who stretch out holes in their earlobes, our resistance to harm and our adaptation to physical pain has brought us pretty far. Our brain, on the other hand, is a complete disaster at ponying up on its end.

For being the epicenter of thought, rationalization, and creativity, the brain is an idiot. Maybe its executive functioning limits its ability to deal with emotions. I guess, in the larger picture, things like breathing and math override hurt feelings and self-compassion. Regardless of my brain's priorities, the things I was bottling up were going to explode one way or another.

I was sad. Maybe sadness was something to focus on rather than dealing with my father's death. Maybe it was a result of the guilt I felt for not being more present in my own life. Maybe it was just my brain finally realizing it had to act. Either way, my sadness was isolating me and making me unbearable. My newfound depression was becoming an issue.

"You know, depression is anger turned inward," Nicole told me, quoting Sigmund Freud. "What are you angry about?"

I thought hard about what she was asking, and even though it sounded general, it was absolutely the truth.

"Everything."

Mediating between the calm presence I needed to be and the proactive, dominant male I wanted to be was creating an internal conflict that left me feeling lost. It was beyond silly rules and habitual emotional hiatuses; it was a raw feeling that was triggered by my paranoia. After a few hard realizations and sessions with Nicole, I concluded that the main antagonists of my anger and fear were social media and the news. I decided, as a New Year's resolution, I would quit all of my social apps and never turn on the news again. Being in the dark is far more productive than living in the dark, and I was convinced that 2021 was going to be the end of my bad run and the end of civilization in general.

I realized quickly after deleting my social media presence that I felt empty, but it wasn't a feeling of missing out as much as it was a feeling of not giving in. I missed interjecting witty retorts and funny memes to friends. I missed faceless arguments with people who I disagreed with on a visceral level, but most of all, I missed being angry.

I missed refreshing my screen over and over as I awaited the next foolish thing someone would say as a counterpoint to the clever thing I just said. I missed the vile contempt I had for friends that became enemies and their twisted logic as I called them names. I missed pointing out the hypocrisy of someone claiming they were an "ally" of some minority group, only to point out publicly that they had no pictures of anyone from that group in any of their photos.

God damn it, I was addicted to being mad.

It's been almost 20 years since my comic, *Bitterman*, debuted in the Fundalini pages of *Mad Magazine*. In 2004, I didn't have a whole lot to be angry about, but I guess my alter ego and creation, Joe Bitterman, was always lingering in the back of my psyche. As I got older and shouldered more responsibilities, had more kids, incurred debt, and did other boring adult things, the more I identified with ol' Joe, and the more cathartic it became to live vicariously through him in the safe spaces of a humorous publication.

With the collapse of *Mad* (and humor in general), it's hard to find an outlet to express ire and irk-ness. So now I do what most people do:

Hold it inside until it is released like a hot geyser because an old lady is driving too slowly or is taking too long to order from the dollar menu.

I'm headed toward the security gate at BWI, and I can already tell that this is going to be an occasion worth getting angry about. I can tell the rotund TSA agent just hates people, as her mechanical expressions are already void of any pleasantries like "thank you" and "have a nice day." I abhor this part of the trip because one really has to take whatever shit they want to give you. Fuck up and play around, and you'll find yourself offering head to any truckers going north.

Luckily, I have my mantra and meds, so I'm ready.

"ID," says Deneequa, the slothy security guard.

"Here ya go," I say gleefully. "How are you today?"

She looks pissed and confused as she looks up and stares at me blankly, trying to find the right response. I smile.

Shit, did I just smile?!

"Step aside, sir, and empty your pockets and present your flight information."

Fuck, I DID smile. "Rookie mistake, Gerhart—now you're going to pay."

RULE: KINDNESS IS BLINDNESS

It's 5 a.m., and I can't believe that I'm getting the shakedown for trying to be nice. It can't be for any other reason than that I am a cis white male who is flaunting my pleasant privilege in the face of oppression. Do terrorists really wear New Balance shoes and carry teal neck pillows? I am sure that no jihadist wants to meet Allah with bunions, and it's probably hard to fuck 17 virgins with a stiff neck—so perhaps?

After a few more questions and a good pat-down, I am forced to bite my tongue and accept the punishment for not matching her misery. I head toward the first gate on the first leg of my journey.

Like a food addiction, anger is harder to control because it's supposed to be a natural response in a well-rounded mental toolbox. You need to eat to stay alive, and you need to experience anger to appreciate peace. So how do you limit your amount of anger?

Is there an anger diet? Keto for assholes?

Whatever was going to help with my anger would have to be done remotely because of Covid. I was used to seeing

Nicole personally, and seeing her via computer screen reminded me that the world was advancing. If movies from the 80s taught us anything, it was that at the very least we wouldn't have to actually go anywhere. Hell, even Marty McFly and Brundle Fly figured out that nothing beats a good teleportation pod and video chat with dickhead Biff Tanner. Sitting across from Nicole during our last session, I felt more at home because I was at home. Nothing helps jog painful memories and heal childhood wounds more than hearing my kids argue about who gets to shit first.

I was surprised at how much Nicole had retained from our prior visits, and I was even impressed at how easy it was to talk to her over time. On our first meeting, I remember her giving me her credentials and specialties. She said she specialized in treating men (check), former military (check), and law enforcement (check). To test her fortitude, I casually said "fuck" in response to one of her questions, and true to her résumé, she didn't bat an eye or shy away. She sat there in her virtual space while allowing me to continue to open up mine.

Remotely, I learned more about my anger, depression, and hope. My sessions with Nicole helped me identify triggers and deal with my emotions before they turned ugly. Most of the time, it wasn't really anger I was dealing with as much as being frustrated with not having the right tools to deal with stress. She gave me homework that would train me to react better to situations like this. Breathing techniques and mindfulness replaced smoking and drinking, but it was still difficult for me to sustain happiness for a long period of time.

The most important thing I have learned in dealing with my anger is that we are tied to those we care about on a deep and spiritual level, and that sometimes I can mistake passion for anger. At times, I come across short or abusive because I want to be heard. I want to make that valid point in a heated argument or stop my kids from running in the house before they get hurt.

Empathy is still a skill that I am trying to learn day to day, but I find that it's probably more real and effective if it's a natural inclination. It's difficult for me to believe that the B.I.T.C.H. from TSA could just be having a bad day—or just learned that her mother has cancer—but I'm trying to be more moral.

CHAPTER
Nine

THE MAN IN 29D

It's 4:30 a.m. on July 1, 2021, and I really wish I hadn't had coffee. I'm at the terminal for my flight to St. Paul, Minneapolis, that boards in an hour. It's not the jitteriness of the caffeine; it's the rancid coffee breath that is congregating in my mask. At this point, I think I would rather take my chances with Covid. If China really wanted to punish us, they should release whatever combination I have wafting in my nose.

Aside from wearing the mask, not much has changed in airports since last year when travel was banned. TSA agents are still dicks, and the angry woman at Dunkin' is still immune to my charms when she asks me if I want my coffee hot, and I say, "I'm already hot."

There's a calmness in early morning flights, which is nice because I am a bundle of anxiety. I'm not so concerned with the plane going down in flames as I am with being late. Because…

RULE: AGAIN, IF YOU'RE NOT EAR-LY, YOU'RE LATE

Late for me is 1–2 hours before the flight, so you can imagine I'm a real joy to travel with.

I like to watch people, and you can really get a good sense of what someone is like at 4 a.m. There are about 12 people at my gate now, and they look clean. One particular lady looks to be a germaphobe as she sits in a crisscross-applesauce defensive posture. She's quarantined herself in the middle of a three-seat section and built a fortress with a Michael Kors carry-on bag, Cheez-Its, and Snickers wrappers.

Another young girl is sitting perpendicularly from me and looks to be dressed for some type of Caribbean rave party as she flaunts a hyper-green bikini thing. She looks completely out of place, and I wonder if she's on molly and doesn't know the difference between St. Croix and St. Paul.

I think about what people think of me. I'm wearing an olive T-shirt, blue jeans, tennis shoes, and a new Stetson Stratoliner that I got a few weeks ago. I don't know if I'm trying too hard to be something I'm not, or fit into a persona that reflects the working me. I rationalize my wardrobe as functional for the Montana environment. You never know when a rattler is going to spring out of the sage and bite at your legs. Now, aren't you glad you wore boots? The sun is hot, and what am I going to do—wear a faddish Patagonia hat like a suburban asshole?

Fuck it. I'm 46 years old now, and middle-aged me is entitled to wear what I want (unless my wife says otherwise). I'm also entitled to start calling women in their 20s "Darlin'" and "Honey" without fear of remorse and retribution.

I don't know much about this first leg of my trip. I can't recall ever going to St. Paul—or Minnesota, for that matter. The only thing I know about Minnesota has something to do with *Laverne & Shirley* and *Happy Days*. I may be confusing my Garry Marshall productions, but based on the convoy of pasty passengers waiting with me, I would guess that there aren't many progressive sitcoms based in Minnesota.

I'm flying out of Baltimore to my final destination, Bozeman, Montana. Much like Minnesota, I don't know much about the state of *Oro y Plata*. I only know that I had to Google what *Oro y Plata* means (gold and silver, for the continentally challenged), and that no one ever says, "Montana? The Big Sky State? Fuck that place!"

Baltimore, on the other hand, is a real shithole. I've tried my best to acclimate to this region, but it's impossible. I have friends who live in "the city" and swear that it's a great place to live—as long as you stay away from certain places. Imagine if that mentality converged with any other aspects of your daily life.

"How was grocery shopping?"

"Great, but I almost got lost and wandered into the dangerous frozen food section."

"What did the doctor say about your high blood pressure?"

"I don't know; he put his finger in my ass and sent me on my way with a lollipop and his phone number."

Since I really can't call any place my hometown, I guess I'm cynical and a little bitter about people having roots. I've never considered myself to be part of any community, nor have I considered myself a nomad. I think I attach to people. I find that it opens your options exponentially—from just 50-plus—and gives you a greater degree of control and selectiveness. The problem is that people leave, and when they do, you're a man without a country, floating in the ocean until you wash up on another living island.

The more I think about going to Montana, the more I think it's about going back to the people. The people who knew me. The people I forgot, and the people who I am anxious to meet again. I hope that when I land and step outside without the cotton-roasted, coffee-infused mask, I am greeted with a sound or scent of something that triggers a feeling or distant memory. I hope that I am hugged, and a wave of nostalgia hits me so deeply that everything comes back in an instant. I hope that the people I meet, the things I learn, and the experiences I share give me footing in a place that offers peace and comfort.

I hope that I feel home.

They're calling my row to board now, and the old man next to me is giving his friend his take on same-sex marriage, and all I can think of is a 2021 version of a gay, biracial *Laverne & Shirley*.

God,

kill me.

CHAPTER

Ten

THE FALL

No, really, God. Kill me.

January 28, 2021, 9:50 PM:

"I don't know if what I want is too far away or if I'm too far gone. The only thing I do know is the abyss of failure that I live in like a slothy agoraphobe. I think about ending it all. I think about how I would do it in a way that would be easiest for my family. There's no way to do that, so I would end up failing at that too. Maybe when my wife realizes that she can do better and leaves, and the kids are grown up, I can do it the way I want. Alone in the woods. Gun under chin. In the fall. I want the last thing I feel to be cold air. I feel so empty and occupy nothing. I think I've always felt this way, but I was young and active enough to displace that feeling with other things. It's very hard for me to consistently be present, and I don't think that's how we're meant to live. Maybe we're supposed to look forward to the future while embracing the past, but I don't even do that. I'm just stuck in the present without being present, and it makes me feel like a ghost. I have moments of it, I think. I was proud of my son today as he interacted and learned from older kids. I'm always proud to see Jenny growing and being better. I smile at the goofy things my girls do and the bond they share. But these moments are at the expense of other people, and I feel bad for latching onto them. I'm going to go to bed now. Maybe I'll have a heart attack and die in my sleep. I'm so pathetic that I need a machine to help me breathe at night. Imagine that."

I haven't read this passage from my notes section— much less written about it—since I first created it. Even after all the therapy and progress I have made in the past few months, I am still ashamed and afraid of it.

I think what made it so bad was the fact that I was doing everything right. Therapy had given me tools to address my anger and depression, and my family was supporting me in becoming better. I didn't lack compassion or love from them, and that's what made it worse.

I had failed.

It was a string of failures. It started with losing a few of my regular gigs because I just wasn't in the right mind space to do great work, or the opportunities simply vanished going into the second year of a global pandemic. These few annual jobs counted for about 80 percent of my annual salary, and all at once, they were gone, and a big, big unbreakable rule was broken.

RULE: BE A MAN

I had a drill sergeant that once told me, at the end of my basic training, that there was one rule to being a soldier. He wasn't the typical alpha-male, swinging-dick drill sergeant that you see in movies; he was more like a satire of that archetype. He was what I imagined happened to solid soldiers if they got wet and ate after midnight. He often appeared drunk, belligerent, sweaty, and only showed up at strange hours and days. Hell, I may have reached fatigue from the Kentucky sun and constant ruck marches, and he may have just been in my own head.

Regardless, he took a liking to me because I was always fucking up and doing some remedial training when everyone else got to take a break. I think we shared this bond and schedule. While sweeping a long stretch of sidewalk on a Sunday afternoon while my friends were listening to the new Pearl Jam album, he approached me.

"Yes, Drill Sergeant!"

"Do you know what the secret of life is?"

My mind came up with several clever quips, but I maintained discipline so as not to sweep any more sidewalks.

"No, Drill Sergeant!"

He looked around at where I started and how much further I had to go and shook his head to signal a compassionate reverence.

"Get your shit done and fuck off."

I wasn't sure if he was dropping some backwoods Kentucky wisdom from a bottle or giving me an order.

"Got it, Gerhart?" he inquired.

"Ummm, I think so," I proclaimed.

"It means just be a fucking man," he said, as he strolled back to the comfort of shade and into my psychological hall of fame.

For over 20 years, I carried that nugget with me and used it as the litmus test of how a man should think and act.

Wanna go to college? Get your shit done and fuck off.

Wanna start a family? Get your shit done and fuck off.

Wanna start a new career? Get your shit done and fuck off.

Wanna get your mind right? Get your shit done and fuck off.

For me, "get your shit done and fuck off" was an easy-to-attain mantra that was straightforward and so obvious that I can't believe a professor of psychology hasn't titled a book like that. It was a foolproof motto that had gotten me far in my family, career, and my first round of therapy. I put in the work, and now I should be rewarded.

But what happens when your identity as a man—husband, father, protector, provider—is so rigidly directed and motivated by a two-part life thesis? What happens when you get your shit done, but the fuck-off part never comes? It's supposed to. That's what makes the phrase so impactful. It's just two steps.

It's easy not to feel like a failure when you successfully put together a Huber Norfurn from IKEA. For fuck's sake, before NASA clears you for the space program, they probably test your ability to assemble a Nermerplog in under three hours. Anyone should be able to execute a two-step plan—especially one that was handed down personally by Sergeant Shangri-La, who walked it down from the Mountain of Enlisted Enlightenment.

One hundred years ago, a man would show his fortitude and success with how much wood he could carry home to cook the animal he just killed, in a pelt he was wearing from another animal he killed. Nowadays, a man flaunts his contacts on his newest iPhone and lines of crypto credit that he used to buy tickets to Bonnaroo. The vessels have changed, but the direction is still the same.

If a man can't provide for his family, is he still a man? Within the last few months, I had lost my temper, my mind, and my work. Everything that my perception, history, and biology told me was gone. I wasn't stoic like the men in the movies Pops took me to. I wasn't providing in the sense that generations of men before had, and I sure hadn't slain any emotional demons like I thought I had.

I tried to take solace and refuge in the things that they say matter in life. Ask any guru and spiritual advisor, and they all come to the same existential conclusion. Life is a journey, blah blah blah. A man who has the love of others, yada, yada, yada. Empty and vague affirmations that bear no fruit when you're in the thick of it.

I hear people say that suicide is selfish, but I don't think that's true. I think the events that lead to that final decision are selfish. There is a period of "self" that is so heightened when you're at your lowest.

Self-Aware:

I know that everyone will be better off without me.

Self-Destructive:

It will all be over soon, so why not indulge in the few things I enjoy?

Self-Reflective:

I am causing this pain. Without me, there will be no pain.

Self-Fulfilling Prophecy:

I don't matter.

You become so repetitive and tormented that it feels like life is a never-ending roller coaster that is void of anything that would make the ride fun. There are no lights, no sounds, no reference of space. It's just a dark and clunky, jerking experience that is designed to make you so sick that you would do anything for it to stop. Getting off becomes less about self-destruction and more about self-preservation. The only way to stop being selfish is to get the hell off the ride.

I hadn't committed to any plan, but there was a redundant feeling of hopelessness. I had never been a person to surrender to negative thoughts. In fact, I go out of my way not to experience them at all. If I think my credit card statement is going to make me panic, I won't open the bill. When my family and friends pass away, I don't go to their funerals. I think that by not gradually experiencing loss and sadness, it made the impact of my depression worse.

The only lifeline I had was that I still considered myself to be a good father and a stable husband.

When you go (back) to therapy after having suicidal thoughts, it becomes a minefield of what you want to disclose and how much you're willing to sacrifice. As a man, you must decide what control you're willing to relinquish to become a better person.

I never told anyone about it, and I think that is a big reason why I couldn't go through with it. The thought of ending it all was repetitive and warm, and ending the hopelessness was the only thing that I found hope in.

I was stuck in that mindset like a mouse in a glue trap. The harder I struggled to get out, the deeper and stickier I sunk. I couldn't move, and the struggle sedated me. That's probably what ended up saving me.

Like that mouse, I just had to slowly lose hope in a dark corner until someone found and disposed of me.

For months, I lived in torment and hid.

I was depressed about being depressed and angry that what I had wasn't good enough for me. An emotionally and financially supportive wife afforded me the opportunity to focus on my mental health. I had five smart and healthy children and a job that I could walk away from until I felt ready to return. I had every advantage to find my footing and get better, but when the focus became on myself, I became tangled in negative self-talk and self-destruction.

"I have it pretty good. Why am I meant to suffer?"

"Anyone would kill for the life I have!"

"They deserve better than me."

"They would all be better off if I wasn't around."

On a seemingly uneventful day, as my wife and I were driving back from some menial tasks, I told her. There was no reason to tell her; the subject wasn't brought up, and there was no trigger that made me that vulnerable.

Over the past year, Jenny could see the solemnness in my eyes, and she had known that I hadn't been myself. She was never satisfied with my common answers of "I'm fine" and "I'm just tired." She knew I had to come to my own realization to ask for help, so she quietly waited for me to take the first steps and reach out.

We sat idle in our car at an intersection we had sat at

many times. Since this intersection was two minutes from our home and a light we could never seem to catch, we usually spent the time constructing our game plan for the day or figuring out what we were going to cook that night. It was an impasse for near-future planning. Ironically, this is the spot I told her, "I need help."

"What can I do?" she asked.

"Nothing," I said. "There's nothing anyone can do."

CHAPTER
Eleven

THAT TO WHICH I KNOW

I t seems the farther you get from the U.S. coastline, the closer you get to humanity. Even from the Minneapolis Airport C Terminal, I can look out and see some raised land features that seem like they can ground and direct you physically and spiritually. I am surrounded at the gate by denim and talk of trucks and breakfast. I am confident that Bozeman will bode the same fare, and I will feel a sense of home.

Delta flight 2440 from Minnesota to Bozeman has all the whistles and perks. Sure, we thought we would be flying cars or transporting them to these places by now, but having the conveniences of Wi-Fi, imported beer, and an 8-inch touchscreen with free movies and games is a close second.

I estimate that there are over 80 screens on this flight, and I can't help but think of my father-in-law's obsession with EMFs. I wonder if he would walk out or try to convert the ignorant masses to his plight of eliminating harmful radiation that causes cancer and autism.

RULE: FATHER KNOWS BEST

Every so often, when he comes to visit, he brings articles and an EMF detector to point out the high-risk areas in our house. He warns us that having the router on all day will eventually give us brain tumors.

Even as I type this, with my laptop near my testicles, I squirm thinking about the invisible energy that will render my penis useless and soil my sack with massive knots that would make the thalidomide kids look like the Kardashians.

My wife's father means well, as I suspect all fathers do. I think about his obsessive nature, his rules, and how much stress it brings. I wonder if it's a learned behavior, like riding a bike, or if it's as natural as breathing. I wonder what he would do with his time if he weren't so protective. I think about my own issues as a father. I look back on the choices I made—some out of inexperience, some out of fear, some spontaneous, all out of love.

My Pops was and is the model from which I learned the trials, pains, and joys of fatherhood. Adopting me at the age of eight, we both went in as novices and learned boundaries, as well as love and acceptance, in a careful and clumsy state. It was because of his openness to loving me and my mother that I decided to take on his last name and carry his legacy as his only child.

We had a blast growing up together. He was a good man who could always bring a smile to my face, and I knew that he loved my mother. I remember cheering him on as he tried to find out how many Taco Bell tacos he could eat in one sitting. Not to be outdone by that feat, shortly after, he would try to beat the record for how fast he could light his farts on fire. It was, after all, Mexican food.

Perhaps his greatest gift to me—one that can't be shared through genes or passed down from family—is a love of pop culture. When he met my mother in 1982, he was with an outfit based out of Grand Junction, Colorado, called

National Cementers, who I assume had something to do with concrete. When he was dating my mom, he would take me on what we called "Tough National Cementers Night Out." These nights consisted of him taking me to most movies of my choice with all the accoutrements that the venue had to offer.

Coke, popcorn, pizza, and candy fueled my obsession with the latest Stallone or Schwarzenegger tale as we bonded over the way a head exploded or the realistic way an alien popped out of a chest. It never occurred to me at the time that there was anywhere else he would rather be than with me. It wasn't until I had my own kids and suffered through summer weekends of ball-sticking sports and soul-less renditions of "Hot Cross Buns" at school recitals that I realized he probably would have liked to spend time with people his own age.

It was on one of these nights out that I noticed my first woman. I mean, I had noticed women before as nurturers and disciplinarians. I noticed the way my mother's voice sounded as she drove, singing Christmas carols, and the way her mother told me to stop jumping on the couch. The women I knew were tough. They were from the Midwest, daughters of ranchers, and knew how to drive manual trans-missions. They took long drags on Marlboro Reds and made their children smoke a whole pack if they tried to sneak a drag in the woods with friends.

But when Pops took me to see *Swamp Thing* in a late-night small theater in Grand Junction, Colorado, two partic-ular things about a woman became very clear.

The real hero of *Swamp Thing* wasn't Dr. Alec Holland; it was the costume designer for Adrienne Barbeau. For 40 minutes, this sweaty and voluptuous vixen endured the hazards of the swamp, dodging mutated monsters and the awkward boner of an eight-year-old kid. The white linen dress that stuck to her body would fuel many long showers for years to come and would set a big standard for physical beauty well into my 30s.

According to Pops, I adjudicated this first step into male sexuality by saying, "She sure is bouncy." Sadly, my charm and flirtatious banter haven't changed much since 1982.

RULE: YOU ALWAYS HAVE TO LOVE YOUR KIDS

My mother was a beautiful and caring woman who made me feel special every day until I got older, and it all went to shit. Despite our waning relationship nowadays, I always admired her. She was a fighter and loved to take the path less traveled. Even as a boy, I recognized her independence and, like me, she seemed most comfortable in the present. Growing up alone with her, we didn't have much, but that didn't stop her from investing in herself to be better. She was a champion of higher education and wanted to make a life on her own terms.

After she and my father divorced, she dated. Boy, did she date. Her suitors were my suitors, and these poor bastards had to spend time with me to get close to her. Whatever modest dinners and drinks they had with her, they had to endure kindergarten pick-up and waiting in unfathomable lines to watch *The Empire Strikes Back*.

None of these guys lasted, of course, and we were both content to spend school nights watching TV and traveling abroad during holidays. When we absolutely needed help, my mother reluctantly headed back to Grand Junction, Colorado, to live with her parents.

Her relationship with her parents was strained, but I always found my time with them—especially my grandpa John—full of fun and excitement.

He was like Clint Eastwood doing an impression of John Wayne, and his blue-and-white Ford truck always seemed to smell like gas and cigarettes and looked just as sturdy. He made his fortune in the oil fields of Colorado, Kansas, and

Montana, and according to my mother, his success was at the backend of shady deals and midnight handshakes with nefarious oil barons. This, of course, added to his mystique and probably gave him more reverence to me than was healthy. Whatever he had going on away from home didn't concern me when I helped him feed his cattle, pick apricots from trees, or steal dabs of his pomade to slick my hair back to look like him. Aside from my stepfather, he was the closest thing to a male role model I could get.

My grandmother was a different story. I always found our relationship at a stalemate. I got the feeling that she, my mother, and I never really got along and that our relationship stopped when she left my father. We were all on the deck of a sinking ship that no one was steering, and I think we were all better off. I spent a lot of time with her in her giant house when my grandfather was away and my mother was working. We fell into a good pattern of "You don't dick with me, and I won't fuck with you." It was a strange dynamic—especially having my wife's parents so obsessively but compassionately involved with their grandkids. I didn't think much about it then because I was used to being alone and figuring things out for myself.

When they both passed, my mother never said anything kind about them. Alive or dead, I never witnessed any form of compassion between them, verbally or physically, and the only legacy left to me was that standard.

Pops' parents were amazing people and welcomed me and my mother into their family with open arms. My new grandfather, Poopsie, was a tall, bald man with a giant white beard who found great joy in the routines of morning walks and Hardee's coffee. He reveled in growing a mint garden in his yard and loved taking his grandkids on fast, jolting rides down his modest rancher on Signal Mountain, Tennessee, to the local Kmart at the foot of the city. Pops' mom, Florence, was a quiet woman who didn't talk that much. We didn't share much of a relationship, but I loved her pork chops and the way she was always doting around the house, taking care of things.

When they passed, there was the same pomp and circumstance that came with my mom losing her parents. It seemed more like a footnote to the day's news and less like a celebration of a well-lived life. Looking back, I don't think it was a character flaw, but just a guarded reaction that most baby boomers have.

Douglas MacKay and Latricia Ludwick gave birth to their only son, Garth Douglas Mackay, on October 17, 1974, in Helena, Montana. A year or so later, that family would be broken, and for the next 12 years, I would be shuffled around the country and back to Montana every holiday. They were, in some ways, the new iconoclasts of the great suburban myth of sticking together and seeing it through. The rebellious '60s proved that women could be independent, men could fold their own clothes, and a few cross-country Christmas kids like me just stood on a cold tarmac waiting for their flight back home. Maybe I'm still that same kid now, but with lower back problems and a mortgage.

I don't remember much about that time, and I don't think it was just because of the divorce. A few of my friends had divorced parents, and they can recall their third-grade teacher and the first time they called daddy's lady friend "New Mommy." I think the boomers were in the shadow of the great feats their parents achieved in the 1940s. Men went to war, and women fought the war at home. Soldiers bled and died in battle, and mothers wiped sniffling noses. Both parents were selfless and didn't abandon their posts. Splitting up and pursuing shinier things was becoming the new metric of independence, and we all suffered. We were told that it was no one's fault that two Christmases would be great—but it was all still so new and absolutely terrifying.

RULE: I'M TOO FUCKING OLD TO HAVE MOMMY ISSUES

The only link I have to the past is with my mother and her bitterness and unresolved issues toward her father and my father, which have spilled over onto me. It's so cliché to sit in a therapist's office and bitch and complain about how you weren't hugged enough or given enough pretty crayons to create a beautiful world, but maybe there is a sad disposition that is carried down like skin color or tolerance to cheese.

Therapy has helped me realize that things will never be "normal" between me and my mother. Healing takes time and two active participants, and I feel like it is too awkward and too late for either of us to be vulnerable. She is a mess, and I'm a mess, and that's about all we have in common. Accepting that certain relationships—albeit mother and son, wife and husband, therapist and client—are based on compromise and respect, I don't see how we can mend bridges when we're both barely treading water.

I'm almost 50. Hell, in a few years I probably will be a grandfather, and the fact that I am still having unresolved issues with my mother makes me feel like a scared child. How can I sustain and nurture any relationships when the first relationship I ever had is broken?

Sure, we share the occasional empty "hellos" and calls at holidays and could probably pass as civil during the occasional face-to-face meeting, but our timing and feelings always seem to be guided by blame and mistrust.

But still, I love her, and that pull for some type of reconciliation is strong—especially since I know what my life could have been like without her.

CHAPTER
Twelve
SON DOWN

There is an older woman sitting next to me with long eyelashes that seem to struggle and bend against the weight of her dark eyeliner. She is from Bozeman. How did I know? Everyone from Bozeman tells you they're from Bozeman—even if you don't ask. Honestly though, it was just nice to sit next to someone who respected my armrest seniority because…

RULE: FIRST COME, FIRST SERVED

"Are you headed to Bozeman for vacation or work?" she inquired as her framed eyes blinked heavily.

"Ummm… a little of both, I suppose."

Eyeliner Lady seemed discontented with that response and waited for me to expound like she was taking my order.

I began to tell her the short version of why and where I was going. I left out most of the key players and some of the context, which probably came across to her as a lie or a sitcom recap. Either way, that didn't stop her from telling me all about Bozeman.

"When was the last time you were in Bozeman?" she asked.

"Jeez, I think I was 12—so 1986?" I asked her, with the subtext of validation.

"Well, just so you know, Bozeman has changed a lot since then. It used to be such a quiet town until everyone started to migrate here from California."

She seemed sad about the decay of the city she had lived in for over 40 years, but also proud that she knew the migration patterns of rich, white elitists and Silicon Valley entrepreneurs.

She was telling me about things to do and places to eat and then pointed out the Rocky Mountains like she was telling me the secret ingredient in her mashed potatoes that made them so creamy. I repaid her kindness and frugal recommendations with an "oh wow," which sounded like a third grader who had just seen his first dinosaur exhibit.

Eyeliner Lady sat back after the Rockies like a woman spent and closed her eyes, falling fast asleep or resting her exhausted charcoal eyelids.

As the plane taxied into the airport, I saw the façade of the terminal and had my first visceral reaction to Montana. No more than two minutes in and already I recognized the brown buildings that made up the airport. It was the same shit-brown paneling that hadn't been renovated since my last trip. The only difference was they added a huge parking garage and used the exact same shit-brown color scheme to make it all blend into a giant shit-brown building. If the Californians were taking over, could they have at least brought offerings of Art Deco architecture—or, at the very least, tempered glass?

The best thing about Montana is that you can immediately get your bearings. It's a wanderer's oasis. A wilderness that you can tame if you take the right path. A place where you can shoot an azimuth within eyeline and feel incredibly small and giant at the same time.

Then I realized the reason why I came. It wasn't to make amends with the past. It wasn't to live in the present. It wasn't even planning a better future.

I wanted to find my bearings.

I wanted to see what came so easily for other people. I wanted to be able to answer the question, "So, where are you from?" I didn't want to stumble and stare into the void when a doctor asked, "What is your family history?" I wanted to look at my aging face and my mental problems and see what *his* baggage was and what I brought on my own.

I didn't want to blame or make excuses like a child; I wanted to learn and know as a man. I wanted to learn about his life so I could improve mine. I wanted the gift that every child wants from their parent: understanding.

My cousin Stacy picks me up from the curb of the modest airport with a giant smile and an old white Ford Escape. I haven't seen her in almost a decade, but I immediately fell back into her presence comfortably.

We are driving 20 miles east to her little town called Manhattan, where she cynically jokes that she's from the "Upper West Side." Stacy Ballard's ambitions for creative success were only matched by her ability to find the majestic in the mundane, and it was her reintroduction that gave me the strength and courage to make the trip with such fluidity. When we reconnected over a decade ago, I immediately liked her. Throughout the years, whenever I fantasized about re-entering the paternal fold, I knew I had to do it gradually and at my own pace. Stacy was—and is—that guide between my life and the life I could have had. I imagine that the reintroduction she initiated through Facebook over a decade ago must have been written and delivered with fear and unknown consequences.

We pull into her rustic home that resides around brick and train tracks. It's a unique, simple place that somehow exists in the middle of town and at the edge of nowhere. The only sound I hear in Manhattan is the gravel popping as we pull into the driveway.

Stacy shares her home with her husband Jason and two foster children, Samantha and Colton. I walk through the doors and see the muted colors of masculinity broken up by pastel palettes that can only be from Stacy and her travels. Only in this Manhattan will you find an antique agate-infused lampshade with a weathered teal statue of Ganesh.

I like it here. I like the simplicity and how everything means something. Stacy points out relics in the house that were my grandparents'. Cupboards of memories and trinkets that have secrets. A place for things out of place.

I meet Jason and the kids, and they are much like the house. They seem to be from here, while Stacy and I feel like visitors. Jason is welcoming and carries himself with a secure confidence that I think comes with residency. Samantha is 14 years old, and Colton is 10. They are both blonde-haired, blue-eyed, proper, and pleasant, and I can't imagine the events that led them to foster care. I am curious but not rude, so I limit my interactions and follow the adults' lead.

Stacy and Jason give me a tour of the property, and it's a testament to home projects and unfinished dreams. There is a fire pit surrounded by benches and chairs welded out of old oil barrels. Dinner is served to the sound of an old cattle bell, even though the yard is only a few hundred feet. There are old car parts and frames of cars that I never knew existed. One looks like a hollowed-out European ice cream truck that is begging to become an all-terrain camping vessel for nomadic retreats in the mountains. Amid the chassis and patches of overgrowth, there is a small Honda motorcycle that Stacy wants to show me.

This particular red motorcycle is a key that unlocked a memory from years ago. During her visit to Maryland, Stacy recalled a story about me and my other cousins riding on a sheet of plywood attached to a similar small red motorcycle.

I had the exact same memory, but I flipped the family to my mother's side and placed the experience on my grandfather's ranch in Colorado. I later found out that the mind can swap locations and people to create a more pleasant and viable scenario. I can't have any good times in an environment so hostile, right?

I sit on the motorcycle and grip the handlebars. Jason asks if I want to take it for a spin, and I refuse. I want to say it's because of some profound existential reason about the dangers of riding down the past, but in all honesty, I'm a fucking klutz, and I fear that my sabbatical will be spent in the ER.

We sit around and compare stories of the East Coast and West Coast. Jason and I share similar geopolitical thoughts and spend our time reminiscing about when states were run better and sharing our ideas on who is to blame and who can fix it. Our banter turns to food and my distaste for anything pulled directly from the Chesapeake Bay. The first victory of our East Coast vs. West Coast battle is made with my first bite of Montana beef at a local pub, and I surrender that free-range Montana beef beats anything from the Atlantic Ocean.

Each state and region can boast their local fare, but the common ingredient that bonds men together is beer. No state, or county for that matter, serves beer any differently. Sure, there are different techniques and formulas, but the basic anatomy is the same, and so is the temperature. Cold, frothy beer is always the start of a good story. It's when it gets flat and warm that the problems usually occur.

We sit for a few hours getting acquainted, and after a few rounds, we are all friends. Samantha and Colton sit at the end of the bar unfazed by the time and occupy themselves quietly and reserved, and I can't help but again feel bad for whatever led them to be in foster care.

We leave full and content on food and memories and head back to the house, where I will take the keys and be pointed in the right direction for White Sulphur Springs. It's almost 3 p.m., and it's still a two-hour drive to my hotel. On the ride back home, I realize that I've had a few drinks on a mostly empty and nervous stomach. I sit in the backseat of the Escape and feel a little lightheaded.

Shit, am I…drunk?

"So, Jason, are there a lot of police between here and White Sulphur Springs?"

He smiles and shifts his glance toward me, and I notice that he's not wearing a seatbelt. "There's no one between here and White Sulphur Springs."

Thirteen

THE ROAD LESS TRAVELED

The last time I remember seeing my father was probably when I was around ten. I don't remember exactly what he looked like, but I remember his voice and the view from outside the car window as we drove back to his apartment in White Sulphur Springs.

My impression of Montana was that it was brutal. The windshield wipers strained under the burden of salt and snow as we left the airport alone, together. Between the heavy streaks came a few moments of clarity, and I remember being in a white emptiness. The roads were as clear and lonely as the heated cabin of my father's Bronco.

Even at ten, I knew the awkwardness that came from our exchanges.

They were always brief, direct, and serious, and it was something that always made me feel disconnected from him. I was in a stable place down in Texas with my mom and Pops. Even though we didn't have much and were living on the poverty line, we were actively trying to build a history with love, routine, and jokes. It wasn't until I was older that I realized most kids didn't eat MREs, and their fathers didn't have to sell blood and plasma so their family could have a good Christmas. Good times!

Time moves slowly as a child. A summer night playing G.I. Joes with your friends or trying to figure out fractions can last forever, and the journey through Montana was no different. The blinding white of the outside created a void of time and space, and I struggled to make the time move faster with silly voices and tales of *Fraggle Rock*. There is a sixth sense that I believe all children of divorce have. It's a deep vacuum that contains the joys and heartaches of each home, and we are conscious and careful not to spill it all out and contaminate the other life we live.

I suspected my father wanted to impress me as I saw him smile through his beard. He sped up around a corner and drifted a bit on the icy road. He could see my smile as I curled my spine closer to the windshield and braced myself against the dash for another round. He repeated the maneuver as I switched into a stock-car, speed-racer announcer voice.

"He's rounding the corner," I yelled. "And he's taking number thirteen. Garth Gerhart is in the lead!"

My father stopped the car. The vacuum that I tried so hard to contain spilled out magnificently as I referred to the alias I was using for the past year. It was the first and only time my father, Doug MacKay, heard his only son, "Garth Mackay," referred to as a Gerhart.

Then he smacked me. I think.

Did I create a violent man to make it easier to detach, or did I detach because he was a violent man? I struggled my whole life to find redemption in my father, and it's snuffed out with memories like this.

Before Karl Gerhart officially adopted me when I was twelve, I remember my father calling my home in Signal Mountain, Tennessee. By this time, Pops had enlisted in the U.S. Army and was accepted into the OCF program, where he would become a 2nd Lieutenant in the Chemical Corps.

This meant more money and better opportunities for our family, but it also meant that he would be gone for a few months of training. We relocated to live with his parents until we got our first duty station.

We spoke casually on the phone, as we usually did, and there was a sadness in his voice. I was distracted by a dinosaur pop-up as we spoke but aware, more than ever, to keep certain news to myself. Whatever plans and schemes the adults were working on were happily kept from me as I rambled on about how big a T-rex could get and how much I was enjoying listening to Billy Joel.

He asked to speak to Karl, which was new and awkward. I held the receiving end of the corded phone tightly and yelled to Pops in the next room, "Dad...my dad wants to talk to you."

My attention to the prehistoric was now on the present as I pretended to hang up, but I secretly listened on the other line. There was a respectful and almost businesslike conversation between the two. Pops's usual jovial voice collapsed a few octaves, and he spoke to my father like an earnest detective on *Hill Street Blues*.

My father spoke, "So, you like my son?"

"Yes, I do. He's a great kid," Pops replied.

"And you want to adopt him?"

"Yes. Yes, I do."

I should have hung up right there. It would have saved a lot of self-hatred and years of therapy.

"How much do you want for him?" my father questioned as casually as someone asking for the price of a cup of coffee.

I smashed the phone down and ripped my book in half with deep anger. This time the smack was real and damaging, and I would spend a lot of time replaying those words and trying to excuse and evaluate their intention. It wasn't that my father surrendered me. I think he knew from my last time with him that I was gone. It was that he surrendered any future with me. I knew from that moment that he would never know any more about me. I would simply always exist in that space he created.

I would never tell him my passion for drawing and creating, my first kisses and inevitable teenage heartbreaks, my successes and vulnerabilities as a man, my failures as a husband, and the joys of being a father.

He, and by proxy we, missed out on moving on and both getting to a better place of understanding and acceptance. We shared similar experiences and weaknesses and had a lot of pain and unanswered questions for each other.

I like to think that our relationship could have been reimagined, and we could have supported each other in our later years. I like to think that I could have confessed to him that I was too embarrassed or ashamed to tell people close to me. I wanted to imagine that I could have helped him find peace and that he could do the same for me. I like to think that we could have traveled a different path together as two broken men just trying to get better without judgment or reservation—but he's gone, and I'm on this road alone.

CHAPTER

Fourteen

GHOST TOWN

They say you can never go home again, and I think that may be true everywhere except Montana. I estimate there are only three roads in this state, so the odds of you finding your way home are almost a mathematical certainty. Maybe that's why it's so easy to get lost everywhere else—there are just too many roads.

I've been on this stretch of highway for over an hour, and Jason was right; there is no one out here. The ride itself is smooth and pleasant. I am told that this particular summer is hotter than usual. When I told the few people I have casually met that I am from Maryland, they jokingly ask if I brought the hot weather with me, and I chuckle. It's only been eight hours or so, and I am hesitant to be too cynical too soon.

I feel free, and I'm not sure if it's the majesty of the fresh mountains, the thin, clean air, or the few beers working their way through my liver. Either way, I roll down the windows a few inches. A few more miles down the road, the windows are completely down, and the radio is howling as I look for something that is clear and contemporary. The closest thing I can find is a static-infused Gin Blossoms song. It's outdated and cliché, but it beats the depressing country songs that seem to come in clear as a bell even deep in the mountains.

In contrast, it's quite a different experience from the last time I was on this road—at least I assume it's this road. It's warm and bright, and I am not deprived of conversation as I belt out "Found Out About You" and wrestle with the anxiety of my internal monologue. I am taking this as a good sign, even though time has stood still, and I swear that I have passed this group of sage bushes and cows before.

Finally, about ninety minutes into the trek, I see a different road. I consult the lovely and reassuring voice of Siri, and she confirms that this is indeed the second of three turns I need to take to get to White Sulphur Springs. I took Stacy's advice and chose this route as not only the quickest way to get there, but also because taking this way I will pass where my father was born. It's a small town called Bradford, and it looks like a dystopian wasteland that shows its colorful charm deeper into the heart of its main street. I pass a mural that is massive and out of place, along with a few boot stores and casinos. I really should stop and at least get a few pictures of this romantic Americana, but I feel that I had forty-plus years of detours, and I'm anxious to put my feet up and pee. Plus, who fucking drops bets in Bradford, Montana?

Making the turn west past Bradford, I'm in another small town called Three Forks. Heading toward White Sulphur Springs, there is a huge structure that looks more modern and gigantic than anything I have seen since downtown Bozeman. It looks like a movie studio that was financed by some big producer for another sequel to *Tremors*, then abandoned after they realized what a stupid fucking idea that would be since Michael Gross is too old to be chasing Grabboids.

I slow down as I pass it and squint against the sun to see the words "Teasers." Fuck, I was close! It's a strip club with an Adam & Eve adult toy store next to it. To the immediate left is a Texaco, and the marketing man in me goes crazy with all kinds of ideas and questions.

"Need gas and a lap dance? Come to Teasers!"

"Teasers, where the only thing between you and hot girls is 120 miles!"

"Teasers—because what else do you have to do in Montana? Try our pure Montana beef and then pork at Teasers."

In my late twenties, I would have had to stop for at least a lap dance. In my thirties, I would have had to stop for a drink. Now I just want to stop to take a piss and see if this is or isn't the place from *From Dusk Till Dawn.*

My thoughts of bad girls and bad choices occupy my mind for a moment, and I realize that miles have passed, and I am once again ironically engulfed between two large mountains.

The closer you get to mountain ranges, the smaller things get, and your perspective becomes blurred. With my ETA coming closer and closer, I feel like I am being devoured by the landscape. The black spots on the mountains that looked like shadows miles away now show the ravages of recent forest fires left behind, and the clean air that rejuvenated my lungs is now stinging my nostrils.

I've seen this damage before—in a dream or in my father's stories. It's a vision that you can't quite make out, so you squint and concentrate until your mind fills in the blank spaces and gives you the narrative. My father was, for most of his life, a forest ranger. I have physical pictures of him on the job, enforcing the laws of men and dressing up as Smokey Bear for children. I didn't know my father well enough to know if he was ever proud of anything, but he was proud of his profession.

Then, out of nowhere and unprovoked, Brooke texts me: "Make sure you stop at the ranger station on the left once you get into town and grab a map!"

Of course—the ranger station! I knew it was on the left and had a huge wooden sign with Smokey Bear on it. I remember the smell. I remember going there as a child and sifting through the tchotchkes reserved from promotions and fairs. I remember sitting at an old, dark desk that smelled like soot and ash and drawing pictures with freshly sharpened neon green pencils. I remember walking through deep snow to get there to spend the day with my father and not dreading the time or company. I can see his beige and green hat with the Forest Service logo on it and how tight the fabric stretched across his big biceps and shoulders.

I am lost in the past, but present as the GPS winds down like a clock. I look at the mileage tick like a call to some new revelation and new beginning. My anxiety is replaced with excitement, and I am confident that the ranger station I knew as a boy is still the one I will see in a few short minutes.

The station and sign are exactly where I knew they would be, on the outskirts of the small town, right after the town cemetery and across from a rustic restaurant. I am so confident in its standing that I turn off the GPS alerts and sail into town sights unseen. The snow caked on the front desk is replaced by gray and brown gravel, and the smell of smoke is erased by a "No Smoking" sign. But there on the sign next to the office is Smokey the Bear.

My eagerness for confirmation turns to dread as I realize it might be closed or renovated. The "Open" sign is a small relief, as I hope that the façade isn't just a façade. I open the door, and there is a friendly, red-bearded man who looks to be in his early thirties. The last time I was here, I was a boy surrounded by the grand wisdom of middle-aged men, and now I am a middle-aged man. I have a good decade on these rangers, and it's odd to be back older than my father would have been.

The area looks smaller than I remember, but most things do through the lens of an adult. Flowerbeds can be an oasis, and fences can be inescapable jail bars when you're a kid, so I forgive my naïveté of scale.

Beyond the modern necessities of forest ranging—computers, cell phones, and Keurig instant coffee—I see the area where I would sit and hang out with the men of White Sulphur Springs. It's cleaner, and everything wood is replaced by smooth textiles and plexiglass. The old, tattered couches are now bright, contemporary pieces that look to double as extra beds should the need arise. The smell of smoldering earth is now industrial cleaning supplies meant to kill COVID-19. I find it bizarre that the biggest danger in this wild region—more than rampaging bears, militant deviants, and bushfires—is probably in this very small office of five adults plus me.

Stacy often tells me that my father's history in White Sulphur Springs is spotty. He was born and raised here and would have died here if it weren't for his standing within the community. I hope to learn more about what he took, what he owed, and what was left as I spend the week here, but for now, I opt to take a low profile.

"You here for the Fourth of July parade or the All-Years Reunion?" the ranger asks.

I wish I could tell him the real reason I am here. I want to tell him, "I'm the estranged son of Douglas MacKay. I need a map of the region so I can find the exact spot to spread his ashes to honor his last wishes."

"The Fourth of July parade," I say.

"Should be a good time, and the weather is going to be perfect!

Where are you coming from?"

"East Coast—Maryland, to be exact," I say.

"Oh, I see," he says with a smile. "Brought some of that hot weather with you, huh?"

"Uh-huh," I say through gritted teeth. "Got a map?"

Less than half a mile down the road is the Spa Hotel. It's one of two hotels in White Sulphur Springs, and it's known for its natural hot sulphur pool, which drains and refills with fresh sulphur water every morning.

I booked a four-night stay here, and true to its name—and void of any cute marketing ploys or gimmicks—the inn surrounds a natural spring whose temperatures reach 105 degrees. The innkeeper, Elvita, told me that I looked hot and that I could enjoy the "cold" spa that goes to a frigid 95 degrees.

I opted for the new suites that come with a complimentary fridge and microwave and are closer to the springs. If you've never smelled sulphur, then you probably can't imagine why anyone would vie for a spot closer. It's a pungent, rude smell that is thick—but at least I have a fridge.

My fight-or-flight reflex passes, and I am finally able to pee and get comfortable for a few minutes. The room is a strange canary yellow and is increasing my anxiety. I have read that some colors can affect your mood, and the longer you stay enveloped in certain colors, the more they can actually trigger panic attacks. When you've had a full-blown mental breakdown, a panic attack is like a cold sore. It's annoying, and you cover it up the best you can and hope that no one notices and questions your choices in relationships.

I am the first "MacKay" to arrive, and I have tonight to venture out alone and see the town. I am grateful that I had the insight to plan some time alone. I want to experience this spot unbiased and uncompromised. I want to walk down the streets my father walked and see things from a genetic and personal perspective. I don't know if there is a pull that guides us that is beyond the present self. Part of my therapy has been learning to surrender and see things as they are, not how I want them to be. For now, I want to walk by what I believe is my father's side.

The town of White Sulphur Springs is literally a one-horse town. It's small, with one main road surrounded by a mix of dilapidated houses and fresh, sprawling businesses looking to capitalize on cheap rented spaces. The government building even has a broken sculpture of a horse that winds and glides with every hard wind rolling off the mountains. It's 6 p.m. rush hour, and it's so quiet that you can actually hear the metal straining and the rust peppering from the metal fowl's joints.

I start to feel lonely and call my wife for a mental pep talk. She is eager to know everything, and the sound of her voice makes me feel like I'm home. I talk to her about the drive in and the sensations I'm feeling, and I start to choke on my words. My throat is rough and dry, and my voice strains to maintain our conversation.

We've talked for about ten minutes and realize that I am at the end of town. I cut the call short, promise to call back, and look for a place to get a drink of water. The closest place I see is a modern-looking bar called the 2 Bassett Saloon. The doors are adorned with illustrations of two bassets drinking beer, and I figure that this is a safe space—like a Chuck E. Cheese for adults.

I check my outfit before I enter and confirm that it is about as standard and forgettable as I hope it is. White T-shirts and blue jeans should be universal camouflage anywhere. The only thing I question is my Stetson hat, but thirst has overcome my shyness, and I'm already sitting at a table with a menu.

The patrons are surprisingly diverse. Although the darkest shade of skin tone is Farmer Brown or Rancher Rouge, there is a wide gap in age and socioeconomic class. The barmaid is a young, attractive woman and seems to be all business, as she has limited conversations with customers aside from, "What will it be?"

She asks me what I want, and out of habit—as a white suburban male married to a Jewish princess—I say, "Can I get a club soda with a lime, please?"

I immediately regret my answer sooner than she says, "Excuse me?"

"Ha! I'm just kidding. Can I get a beer and some tap water?"

I am such an idiot, and I feel like my cover is blown. Luckily, I think her standoffish nature and my awkwardness cancel each other out, and she brings me my order and bill.

I drink my water and then start on the beer. I look out the window and scan the area I just walked. One long street in the middle of Montana. I've been here for thirty minutes, and I've seen the entire fucking town. What the hell am I going to do here for four days?

I look closer and try to become present. There is a therapeutic tool that I use occasionally that brings me back to the moment. I tense up my right arm under the table. I am aware of the pressure in my fist and the swelling sensation creeping up my forearm. I am present for the uncomfortable feeling of blood building in my muscles and the fatigue I am starting to feel. I open my eyes and release the tension in my arm. I focus on the feeling of being relaxed and free of tension. I am grounded now in this moment, and I feel present. The barmaid probably thinks I'm jerking off under the table. Hell, that would work too.

I finish my beer, pay my tab, and walk back toward my hotel. The sun is starting to recede behind the mountain, and the cool air feels refreshing. I look at the shops on the street from the opposite end of town and notice something I hadn't noticed on the way in, facing the bright, setting sun.

There is nothing but bars on this street. There has to be more, right?

Well, yes—bars and casinos. One road and at least ten bars and casinos, but it's nothing like the temptations I am used to being so close to Atlantic City. There is no flash or pizzazz or bright, loud bellowing of bells and crowds. It's an unattractive, unnoticeable ambiance that is built into the town itself, as if it's been there since the beginning.

Curiously, I walk past one of the older establishments called Lane Bar and immediately feel the pull to pony up and the push to stay far away. In most cases, I would have no issue going in and taking a closer look, but there is an intimidation I feel about going inside this place. It's dark and cavernous, even as the sun is setting against the grain of the old oak window frames. I squint to see a small pathway leading into a loud blackness, littered with people on the left drinking and people on the right playing slot machines. Neither side notices or even cares about a wayward stranger encroaching on their space, and it's that lack of awareness that makes me so uncomfortable.

It's getting late, and my body is feeling the effects of jet lag, anticipation, and anxiety.

Day one is officially over.

Fifteen

THE HYDRA

I'm not one for reading because I have ADHD and dyslexia. When I do read, it has to be broken down into small, attainable bites, and it has to have colorful pictures and preferably goofy fonts. If a book does manage to grab my shifting attention, I usually absorb some nuggets hidden in a chapter, but not the overall subject of the book.

I once came across an observation from some obtuse author in some random book that we are all the leads in our own play, and those who come in and out of our lives are the supporting cast. It could have been Shakespeare, or it could have been *Spider-Man*, but that concept always stuck with me, and now I think I must add narcissism to my growing list of mental health diagnoses.

I have too much self-hate to be a narcissist, so I think what appealed to me about that analogy was the lack of commitment and randomness of who comes into your life. If we are just acting our part, do we have any control over who stays and who goes? If we eliminate any responsibility in these relationships, can we also deflect any guilt associated with saying goodbye?

Moving forward with this journey, I think I need to closely adopt this mantra and proceed with caution—expectation or fear—and accept that things will happen as they are meant to.

I'm at the Branding Iron Cafe in White Sulphur Springs. It's a small, friendly cafe that uses margarine instead of butter. They have breakfast platter names like "Roper" and "Two Step," and the bottomless coffee is poured into a brown, rustic mug that reminds me of Sunday mornings with my grandma. People here engage with each other with light banter and warm smiles.

When they see someone they know, they sit with them without invitation or hesitation. The server looks to be in her seventies and moves quicker than any barista at Starbucks. The walk over was about a mile under a giant blue sky and a cold breeze. Aside from a few trucks and the sound of sprinklers, you would think this was a ghost town or the same setting from a David Lynch movie.

The people of White Sulphur seem to like it this way, and I'm still not sure how they feel about me strolling their streets. But there is wisdom here—an eclectic society built on calloused hands and simple pleasures that seems to know the gem they have. Helena is fifty miles west, where they can dine, shop, and live there in minutes because the highway is empty and taunts you to go fast. I imagine I am living among an Aesop fable whose lesson is chasing that which you don't need.

Back home, I don't think I have the moral capacity to think about the people I see every day. They are all cookie-cutter Barbie dolls of a dream life, living in a dream home surrounded by artificial algorithms of what to see, say, and eat every day. In the past twelve years, I have seen more toned asses encased in Lululemon and Escalades cluttered with Peloton logos than I can bat a lash-boosted eye at.

An old Ford truck pulls in from the road, and as the dust settles, I see bright blue mascara painted tribally across the face of a woman with cropped blonde hair, wearing dark flannel. I hear the door—or her joints—squeak from inside and catch the shadow cast by her bullish frame. I think of her in my environment and wonder if she knows how wonderfully unique she is and how much I appreciate the change of scenery.

It's good that I am reminded of where I'm at and where I'm from.

The duality of such things, and the mindfulness of what I want to accomplish today, is invigorating—but I am still nervous as hell because there are three women I need to see today. I have a pecking order in mind that will make the meeting more comfortable for me, and if the flow is interrupted, I think I'll be fucked.

It goes like this… Brooke, Kate, Brandi. Or…

Brooke, Brandi, Kate.

Seeing Brooke first is paramount for the whole progression of the day, and I haven't heard from her since getting the map yesterday. I assume that it's too early to text her and ask her to meet. I'm pretty sure she made it in late last night and is now staying in one of the cabins across the street.

I'm not sure how to define and navigate sibling responsibilities, but based on what I've observed from the Kardashians, Olsons, and Huxtables, I think I have some innate responsibility to take the reins and lead the way with seasoned nuance and light teasing.

BROOKE

Brooke is the first daughter of my father and his second wife, Connie. Trauma prevents me from remembering too much about our short time together as kids, but based on old photographs and a few memories, we had a typical sibling relationship. We looked content when we had some space between us and awkward when we were forced to get in close and "smile."

I remember being alone with her and my younger sister, Brandi, for a long time one winter. I don't remember if we were in White Sulphur Springs or another Montana town, but there was wood paneling, brown shag carpeting, and blankets of snow outside. My father had a greying beard, a red turtleneck, and the authority and calm confidence to make it through the storm. He told me he needed to go out for a bit and left me in charge. He said there was beef jerky in the freezer and told me to watch my sisters carefully until he got back. I'm not sure how much time went by, but it was a few days where it was just us.

Brandi was too young to really manage, but I felt a huge responsibility to take care of Brooke and to impress my father. It was my first experience as an older brother, and I have been chasing that feeling ever since. I have an innate desire to "rescue" since that winter, and I think it's all about getting validation from my father and not actually killing anyone. The theme of protector/provider echoed throughout the rest of my life, and it certainly had an impact on my relationships and how I identified as a husband and a father—especially to girls.

Brooke's relationship with my father appears to have taken the opposite side of this dysfunctional spectrum. Whereas I seek to fill the role of patriarch, she has fallen into the role of subservient. Not to say that she is passive, but I sense that she gravitates toward and covets men like my father who are strong, silent, and wrestle with problems.

The last time I saw Brooke was Thanksgiving 2014. We reconnected through social media the way most people connect with childhood acquaintances. We were eager to know everything but kept the conversation light so as not to offend or push too hard or too fast. After a year of casual banter, we made plans for her and her son, Jordan, to visit Maryland—because what's a holiday without a level of unpredictability and cathartic chaos?

Much like the Indians welcomed the Pilgrims to the New

World with a bounty of food and festivities, I arrived at the airport to meet my little sister again. And much like the Indians and Pilgrims, we both were wary of the other's intentions and hoped that, at least for a few days, the savage and the Puritan could coexist and learn from each other.

We spent a few days catching up and allowing each other the space to be comfortable. It was apparent that Brooke idolized my father and that her perception of him was very different from mine. Where I saw a distant and cold man, she saw a warm and loving father. She spoke of his love for his children, but all I saw were stoic impressions of a rough hardness. Our lives were shaped in very different ways by a man who weighed on our existence, and his lack of empathy and joy influenced how we saw our future relationships.

Nevertheless, we were both present and committed to the process of building a new relationship, with years of catching up to do. I was inexperienced as a sibling, and the newly crowned "brother" moniker came with questions and anxiety. I never grew up with anyone, so my compass always pointed where I wanted to go. Some would call that selfish, but it's really navigating the landscape you know. Brooke was raised with her sister Brandi and her older step-sisters, Raquel and Petra. I'm sure her needle danced between the commitments and responsibilities of her sisters and her relationship with her mother and our father, who were now divorced.

Oddly, when we're together or talking on the phone, our compass points toward each other and our paths converge. My self-direction and her compromising ways feel recentered, and we both head toward a destination of unification and understanding.

Even as Brooke told me about my father's ailing health and his ultimate passing, we never veered off course. We weathered the storm in our own way but kept moving forward. That momentum and reliability are why I needed to see her first.

Ironically, at this very moment, as the sun shines high in the Montana sky, I need her to be "Big Brother." I need to see her smile and follow her lead. I need her to make me feel safe on this new path and unfamiliar journey.

Katie

I was freshening up after going with the Roper when the phone rang. Technically, it buzzed, and I only heard it as the last of the vibrations rattled the nightstand. I finished washing my face and heard the buzz again. It was short, so I assumed it was a voicemail from my wife asking if everything was okay.

"Hi, Garth, this is Alena from the Hot Springs Motel. I'm actually in the office, and there's a lady here who would like to meet you. Her name is Kate, and anyway, if you get this message anytime soon, could you swing by or give us a call back? All right, thank you. Bye."

Kate, or Katie, was the last person I wanted to see today. I delayed meeting her because I felt I needed to warm up with a few novice tournaments before our face-to-face, but she knew I was here, and not seeing her now would make it worse. I tied up my boots, said a silent prayer, and made my way past the springs to the office. I made a right through the doors and took the long corridor to the front desk.

As I approached, I saw a small, older woman sitting on a gray couch. She wore a bright blue top and had short gray hair that looked like Van Gogh brush strokes. She turned her head, saw me, and we locked eyes and smiled. As I got closer, she stood up and pulled me in. Her five-foot frame grabbed me tight, and she gave me a giant kiss on the cheek.

"You look just like your dad," she said.

"It's so nice to finally meet you!" I blurted out, dodging her compliment and trying to keep the tempo of our conversation in the present.

You never know how deeply someone can stare at you until you realize they are waiting for someone else to come out of you like an exorcism. She was nice enough, but I kept feeling like I was supposed to say something that would reconnect some dots and give her one extra moment with my father—or maybe my compass has recalibrated, and I'm going back to myself.

Sitting with Katie on that cracked vinyl couch in the middle of a dusty lobby, I know that I'm at a major disadvantage, and that's why I feel so exposed. She knows everything about me. Either from my father, Brooke, or Facebook, Katie MacKay knows all about my past and present. I think about how I can get the upper hand and how I can direct the intimate discussion back to her. I then understand that I know nothing about her, and my stoicism turns to regret.

I do know something about her, though. She's persistent.

For years she tried to connect with me while my father was still alive. Every time I logged onto Facebook and saw the "Katie Mac is awaiting your friend request" button, I would tense up and panic to the point of denial—until denial turned into disregard, and disregard turned into complacency. It wasn't a fear of Katie herself; it was the direct line she had to my father that scared me. Reaching out to her was reaching out to him, and I was in no way equipped—mentally or pharmaceutically—to take on that shit.

I want to be present through this, and presently I am sitting with a woman who probably knew a man at his most desperate and broken, and that is who I wanted to know.

"Have you eaten breakfast yet?" Katie asks.

"No, I haven't," I lie.

"Great! My sister is with me, and we saw a cute little place called the Branding Iron Cafe we are dying to try."

"Let's eat," I say, knowing that the odds of me having another Roper and gastric bypass surgery are in my future.

Katie's sister, Laura, is a nice lady and complements Katie's sporadic, post-stroke personality with a calm and candid manner. I go to shake her hand, and she pulls me in for a big, stuffy hug. It's not as anticipated as Katie's, but I'm getting used to squeezes and the smell of Ben Gay and magnolia body spray.

The café is crowded now as more White Sulphurians reluctantly awaken from their Coors Light covens and grease up their bellies for another night of debauchery. We squeeze into a corner section, order our meals, and get to the point of this whole trip.

Laura's direct approach is probably best suited when talking politics and reconnecting families. She's like the tough-love critic on a talent show who tells the ambitious blonde with big breasts and a raspy voice that she should keep her sights on performing for the deaf. She cuts through the minutia like my serrated knife cutting through my second helping of plump pork sausage.

Sweet Jesus, I'm going to die.

Talking to these women is entertaining and enlightening, as they each have their own unique takes and impressions of my father. Laura tells me that my father loved cats and football. She and her husband would always spend time with Katie and my father, and they enjoyed the occasional drinks over polarizing political talks. My father's conservative ideology didn't quite mix well with their progressiveness, and it occasionally caused a few fistfights.

Fascinating!

Katie sits quietly and intervenes when something pops up or is influenced by one of Laura's observations.

"You know, when your dad stopped working, he wanted to walk out into the ocean and never come back," she interrupted.

"What? Like kill himself?" I asked.

"Well, he just lost purpose when he stopped working and didn't want to be around anymore," she said, staring out the window.

"Now THIS is what I came all this way for!" I thought. It

was the first time I ever felt a real connection to my father. We shared pain, frustration, and hopelessness like most fathers and sons share DNA or hot dogs at football games.

The shuffling of feet goes quiet as Katie becomes conscious of herself and what I want to know—what I need to know.

"Your father was a good man, but he had his problems," Katie said, as Laura fell silent and looked at Katie for emotional support. I think about how and if anyone has ever said that about me.

"Do you know how we met?" she asked. "We met at a casino while your father was living out of his car. We met at a slot machine when we were both regulars. He was so handsome and persistent in getting to know me. We spent so much time together drinking and gambling, and after a few weeks, I moved him in with me."

"So, he was homeless?"

"Well, he had a home in Montana, but he had a warrant out for his arrest, so he lived out of his car in Oregon when we met. He sold his car to pay off some debts and then stole it back that night and never went back to Montana."

Jesus fucking Christ, who the hell was my father? I mean, I feel validated in a way, but finding out that the man responsible for my existence was capable of such a thug life really questions my own traits and behaviors.

We all sat in silence, and it felt like Katie had said too much and now I knew too much. Thank God for Laura.

"Well, we have to go get ready for the day. Can we see you after we get settled?"

"Sure," I said. "I think I could use a rest too. Maybe I'll check out the hot springs."

Even though I appreciate Katie's honesty and passion when speaking about my father, Laura seems to sense that we don't have all weekend, so she conducts these meetings well. If she is a Wikipedia page, Katie is the underlined text that takes you to another page if you want to know more. I find that this way of absorbing information is direct and more digestible.

Speaking of digestible, it's 11 a.m., and I haven't shit yet. I am going to die.

Brandi

I walk back to my motel, and the smell of sulphur from the pool is not as strong as I approach. I guess I am adapting to the smell, and I start to worry about what else I may be adapting to.

I need a drink. It's not even noon, and I need to escape. I promised myself and everyone else—from my wife to Nicole —that I wasn't going to drink too much while I was here, but after learning about how desperate and sad my father was, I think I deserve a cocktail. I don't know if it's this town, the honesty of the last hour, or the poisoned genetics in my body, but I need to regroup with something that can help calm me down. I honestly don't know how sober people handle problems. I don't even have cigarettes anymore, and the whole "going at it alone" is really starting to get old.

As the internal debate begins, my phone goes off.

"We're at the cabins. Where are you?!" The text tickles my pocket.

Brooke made it in—just in the nick of time. I redirect my struggle to the text and fumble to answer it immediately. I would have been horrible at dating during the age of iPhones and social media. My impulsiveness is like a dog that loses control upon hearing a squeak from his favorite toy. I have no self-control in most of what I do, especially when it comes to relationships.

"On my way!" I eagerly respond like an impetuous asshole.

My stride widens, and my heart rate quickens as I liter- ally bust into the cabin, a lot like an emotionally overflowing Kool-Aid Man.

Brooke and her boyfriend, Cal, are in the middle of

unloading their truck as my nephew Jordan begins his weekend of watching the *Star Wars* marathon in a cold, dark room. We see each other, and I can already tell I'm way more into this meeting and upcoming embrace than she is. I really need to calm the fuck down, as I am the sole representative of the East Coast—which is something this town has probably never seen.

Brooke and I hug and smile at each other, and I feel content, overwhelmingly relaxed, and back in control. Like this town, it feels like time has broken down, and we are relying on echoes of the past and mindfulness of the present to plan the future.

Cal finishes loading out the last of the weekend haul and shakes my hand. His callouses are rigid, but his smile is warm, and I appreciate the integrity of his inclusiveness and patience with my sister. I'm sure a man who drives a Ram truck and uses koozies on his beer can think of several other things he'd rather do during Independence Day weekend than search for feelings with a man he doesn't even know.

I walk into the cabin and say a quick hello to Jordan. I met Jordan once before when he and his mother visited me in Maryland. He's a quiet kid that people say looks a lot like my father. I wonder how that makes Brooke feel. We discuss our favorite episode of *Star Wars*. He says his favorite is *Empire*. The kid is going to be all right.

"Brandi is going to be here soon," Brooke casually mentions as she loads a case of Coors Light into the fridge.

"Oh, that's awesome," I say reluctantly.

I really don't know much about Brandi. She was young—maybe five or so—when I last saw her. Brooke and I barely had a relationship at that time, and Brandi was just a pretty decoration to me. A picture you see on the wall every day that fills a room but you never notice until it's gone. I never knew much about her as she got older. Even with social media, we never reached out to each other, even as Brooke and I were mending our relationship. I'd see her posts and pictures but had no interaction—just decoration.

I have no feelings or expectations in seeing Brandi, and that's a good thing. I appreciate and purposely adopt the same tactics in addressing the past. Everything is clearer at arm's length, and if it stays in the past, then why bother at all? Maybe we have more in common than anyone.

Brooke, Cal, and I are sitting in the cabin's common area, which is a partially shaded haven where booze and cigarettes seem to be the shared tokens of friendship, based on the used butts and bottle caps overflowing in the ashtrays and concrete crevices. Anything different wouldn't complement the aesthetic I've become accustomed to, so I christen the moment by partaking in a can of Coors Light with my new family—Dale Earnhardt koozies added, of course.

After a few sips, the rumbling of tires breaks through the cabins, and a white Toyota RV tears into the space behind Cal's truck. A cloud of dust plumes toward the cabin, and Brandi steps out like a rock star's encore. She is strikingly unique, like Brooke. Blue eyes break through the dark circles around her eyes, paired with an attitude that is neither imposing nor approachable. Dirty blonde hair is matched with a dirtier mouth as she yells out to Brooke, "Where the fuck are you?"

"Over here!" Brooke signals to Brandi as she wades through the weeds along the most direct path to our common area.

Brandi seems to be avoiding any kind of contact—physical or eye—and I find the juxtaposition between her and Brooke interesting, as they are two sides of the same coin.

I make the first move toward Brandi as I get up from my wooden chair swing and meet her at the opening of our makeshift gazebo. We stare silently at each other for a moment as we both anticipate the next steps and hesitate to overstay any kind of first contact.

Brandi's boyfriend, Bryan, is in tow, and now I really feel outmatched. Each pair—even Katie and Laura—are allies for what's ahead tomorrow. Good or bad, it's another sign that I am doing this all for me.

We pull in close and give a friendly hug, exchanging quick banter about her trip and the days ahead. We both catch ourselves about to engage in something deeper but resist as we take our seats and use Brooke as a buffer.

Bryan is a quiet man and has a calming presence about him. He's a rancher around my age, and I can't imagine the turn of events that brought him and my youngest sister together. He follows Brandi's lead, and I'm not sure if it's intentional or a predetermined plan to let Brandi experience this time without distraction. Either way, Bryan is very engaging as he asks me more about myself, and I can't help but notice that Brandi's attention is subtly pulled more toward me with each answer.

I am perplexed by Brandi's aloofness as she interrupts drags from her Camels to engage cynically with Brooke and Cal. I'm concerned that she remembers something hideous I did as a kid or harbors resentment toward me for not being more present in my father's life—especially at the end. There is a history with everyone here except me, and it's evident with each laugh and tear shed. I am watching some weird reality show, and no one knows I'm here.

After a few beers, I settle in and revisit my intentions and challenge my rules. Every instinct and pattern of my personality wants to disengage and disappear into the drink. I want to vanish into a stagnant vessel that says just enough to be witty and lovable when I'm drunk. I've done that with strangers, and before I know it, it's last call and time to go home. It would be so easy to do the same with family.

Brooke offers me another beer, and I decline. I see her offering the same gesture to my father. I see him taking the beer, and another, and then walking to the nearest casino. I see him carelessly shoving his retirement into the gullet of that bottomless hole and losing everything. I see him owing money, not paying, running, and hiding. But most of all, I see him at the edge of the Pacific—the sand under his feet as he walks with what pride he has left toward his end.

"No thanks," I say. "I've had enough."

Sixteen

WE ALL FALL DOWN

The last time I spoke to my father was in the winter of 1998. I have a lot of trouble recalling dates, so I use a very scientific measure to calculate time and space. I had just bought *The Nutty Professor* on DVD, and "Tubthumping" by Chumbawamba was making me want to walk into traffic. It was also the day before I left for Korea.

I had just been promoted to sergeant and had quickly been assigned to the 142nd MP Company in Yongsan, Korea, and I was moving out of my cozy, wood-paneled abode in Killeen, Texas. I wasn't worried about being in a "hostile" environment because of my time at Fort Hood. If anything, it might actually be a break.

The phone rang just days before I was getting my service cut. I heard a deep voice say my name like a principal calling in a troubled student.

"Garth, this is your father."

I sat down on my broken-down bed and immediately wanted to make him proud. There was always a formal annotation in his voice that seemed misplaced on me. I have assumed since we both grew up without each other, he fell back on the same tone he would use with his colleagues or the refrigerator repairman. It's strange that no matter how old we get and how many times we are hurt, we always want to make our parents proud.

"Oh my God, Dad… you won't believe where I'm going! I got promoted to—"

"Son,

I need $500."

He cut me off, and I did the same in turn. I hung up the phone and continued to pack my belongings. What I couldn't pack in two duffel bags, the Army would provide me. So I left him there, in that dusty apartment bedroom, for the rest of his life.

RULE: LEAVE THE PAST IN THE PAST

"Your father loved you" is something that I would hear throughout my visit to Montana. Two of his four wives would tell me how much I meant to him and how proud he was of me.

On the Fourth of July, as the parade of old cars and local businesses moved through the streets, so did the accolades of my father's love from cousins and aunts that I now knew better than I knew him.

"You look just like your father" is something I heard from his old friends and grief-stricken daughters.

"You walk like him," whatever the fuck that means.

Years later, I guess I was still angry. Not at him, or myself, or anyone in particular—just angry. I felt the anger you feel at someone who spoils the ending of a movie by yelling, "Oh, he's dead too," or someone who reneges on a bet. It's an annoying anger that you can't confront because it lives in the past. For whatever turn of events, karma, or nihilistic meaning, you just have to live with it.

So the journey now is about acceptance, I guess. I hate that word—*acceptance*. Does it imply fundamental failure or a cathartic move toward mental healing? Did I sacrifice time, suffer a mental breakdown, and contemplate killing myself for acceptance? Well, that is fucking weak.

All that digging around and opening old wounds, just to say…

RULE: IT IS WHAT IT IS

After the last round of horses galloped by and took a figurative and literal shit in front of me, I felt defeated. Two days of walking around in a town with one street and nothing but bars and casinos.

Maybe it was our national independence that warranted celebration—or maybe it was my impulsive nature—but I started to feel the pull of cold beer and the hot neon lights of the slots. I wanted to go to a better place. I wanted to make a story that wasn't a middle-aged man finding peace. I wanted to make another story of fun and chaos and bad choices and regret. That's a story worth telling. No one gives a fuck about Bukowski window shopping or Hemingway eating a breakfast burrito.

Before I left, I had an honest conversation with my wife. I know what I'm capable of doing to hurt her and the hell I'd have to go through to get her back.

The least dangerous and more acceptable addiction is food. If I couldn't drink myself to sleep, at least I could pass out from the Montana meat sweats. Do I eat at The Lane Bar, The Stockman Bar, or Bar 47? I suddenly realized that this town has no restaurants. This was a town of bars and bar food.

Then a realization came over me as I contemplated the lesser evil. The town of White Sulphur Springs was an oasis of addiction. Not only was every other building in this one-road town a bar or a casino, it was an escape. It was a remote destination where you go to lose everything, and no one would notice—not family, not friends, no one. The isolation of addiction would only pass if you *needed* to be found.

"Hey, I NEED another drink."

"I NEED help standing up."

"Son, I NEED $500."

This was the first time in my life I understood my father. It wasn't pity; it was a deeper understanding of the addictions we had in common and the temptations we shared. For him, living, learning, and working in White Sulphur Springs meant he could never leave. There were roads out of that town, but it must have always been in his rearview mirror.

I thought about other addicts and how similar their existence might be. A drug addict in a meth lab, a smoker in Marlboro County, a pedophile at a Boy Scout jamboree—all would be a strange and wondrous purgatory of pleasure. Why would they want to leave? How could they be virtuous when they are predisposed and exposed to addiction every day?

My father is described as "a man's man," which means his rules must have been more structured and fucked up than mine. From what I've gathered from most peers and knowing what I know about being a man, the basic and hardened rules to being a man are the "3 F's."

1. Feed me
2. Fuck me.
3. Shut the fuck up.

Why complicate things, right? Three simple rules are easy to remember and even easier to practice. They are egotistical and uncompromising. How simple would life be if we all could follow this type of basic strategy?

"Feed me" encompasses the basic necessities to survive, "fuck me" feeds the id and pleasure receptors, and "shut the fuck up" eliminates conflict. Each rule is designed to remove personal responsibility and the ability to adapt and learn from your environment.

My father definitely had a gambling addiction, and I'm

pretty sure he was a functioning alcoholic too. People who knew him are hesitant to give him that label. I hear, "Yeah, he liked to go out and have a few drinks with his friends after work every day," but no one seems to think that was a problem. Maybe it's an attempt to salvage a man's reputation, because one bad vice is one too many for a man who already has one too many.

I told my doctor a few years ago that I was trying to stop smoking.

RULE: I GET TO HAVE ONE BAD VICE

"Who told you that?" he answered.

Just like my therapist, my doctor pointed out the obvious truth.

I told myself that. I gave myself permission to have a vice. It's not gambling away my life's savings; it's not getting blackout drunk. I bargained with myself to give up many things I enjoy, keeping one.

Another rule challenged and eliminated.

"Jesus, can I at least have sex?" I joked.

"As long as it's consensual and you use protection," he quipped back, and I found joy in my Jewish doctor's answer to a very Catholic question.

I'm sitting in my room, processing the last few hours. I really should be soaking in the legendary hot springs, but it smells especially like shit this evening. I heard that they drain it every night and fill it up with "fresh" water. If the smell is any indication of when that time is, it's around 6:16 p.m. PST. Even if the water didn't smell like Ed Asner's asshole, I would still pass.

It's hot here. Or maybe it's me. I haven't stopped sweating since I got off the plane. I was hoping that the higher elevation, serotonin boost, and facing the Hydra would make the beads disappear, but here I am, doused in perspiration like Ed Asner's underwear.

The sun is going down, and I suppose if I wait an hour or so, I may feel some relief. I'm dressed in the exact same thing as yesterday, and I am thankful for my newfound minimalistic lifestyle. While the other citizens of White Sulphur Springs are deciding which trucker hat goes best with which oversized belt buckle, I'm lying on my king bed, watching *Dude, Where's My Car* on TBS.

It's hard to keep up with the plot as I'm bombarded with

group texts about who is coming and where and when things are happening. Every so often, a new name is added to the text stream, and I grow nervous about interacting with more family. I recognize the latest name, which is Eileen. She is my father's sister and Stacy's mother, and if I'm correct, that makes her my aunt. Awesome! I get to tell my father's little sister why I never spoke to him, saw him when he was sick, or attended his funeral on the day of his memorial.

Fun!

Thankfully, it's just going to be me, my sisters, and their other halves.

I don't want to come across as snooty, but I doubt I need to make reservations at a place that has an "All Firearms Welcome" sign next to the outdoor menu. One of the more modern bars is called Bar 47 and looks homey to me.

It has contemporary branding, modern aesthetics, and a gift shop inside. Bar 47 could easily mimic the bars I'm used to back home if it wasn't for the giant stuffed elk head and the sharp twang of Conway Twitty's greatest hits. Hell, Bar 47 even has a gay guy tending bar. Not even a closeted gay guy—an all-in-your-face gay guy named Steven. Talk about progressive! I know there is a great story there, and since I'm early, I try to have some friendly conversation. I get to his name and where he's from until I see I may be coming across as flirtatious, so I show him a picture of my wife so he doesn't get any ideas. He didn't even ask to see her, and now I feel like I read the situation wrong when I see his disappointment. Rescuing me from any further awkward embarrassment and the possibility of the world's first reverse hate crime, my party comes to my aid and pulls up to my table.

We order our food and have a drink. My plan is to eat what I want and switch between gin and tonic and water and tonic—a safety measure that I invoke with my older daughters so as not to get too drunk around wayward, horny college boys. I figure that if I have clear liquid in a glass with a sliver of lemon and a cocktail straw throughout the night, they'll be none the wiser, and I won't come across as a pretentious douchebag from the big city.

The conversation feels lighter to me now. Maybe my guard is down, or everyone else feels at ease now that we've gotten the awkward reunion out of the way. Whatever the dynamic shift, I'm feeling more and more comfortable and open to the possibility that this whole experience will bear fruit.

I divide my attention between my sisters as they bounce insults off one another and share vivid recollections about their time growing up here. Among the stories was the time the "MacKay girls" rolled into town and cruised the main—and only—road. The boy-to-girl ratio favored the fairer sex, so when my sisters visited my father on long weekends or holidays, they were fresh faces to the boys who wandered the same pastures. One night, a few jealous hometown girls got into it with my sisters, and after a backwoods beatdown, Brooke and Brandi spent the night in jail. At the time, my father was still active as the Forest Ranger and had connections with the Sheriff's Office. They didn't stay in jail very long.

With each memory came another round, and with each round, Brandi became more exposed. The thin smile that suspiciously greeted me was now wide and infectious, and the distance between us closed each time we looked at one another.

I understand Brandi now—probably more than I understand most people I've known for most of my life. I can see the side she puts up and the side she lets down. We are cut from the same stained and worn cloth. I get that the hesitancy we both feel toward each other isn't out of anger, but out of pain. Our walls are up not to keep feelings out, but to keep our own from spilling over.

I never felt that wilting sensation with Brooke. Maybe it's because she is more vocal about her feelings, or maybe it's because she was the child born when things were going well with my father and their mother. Maybe Brandi and I share the burden of being consolation prizes to unfulfilled loves. Maybe we were the last shot at our father's happiness, and it banked off the backboard and went out of bounds. Maybe we were his first and last chance at happiness, and we blew it.

"Do you smoke?" Brandi says as she pulls out her first cigarette since dinner.

"I used to," I say. "I'll go out with you if you want some company."

We head out to the front of the bar, and she swipes her hair back while the cigarette dances dialectically from her lips. I begin to understand that I never appreciated the nuance of managing a conversation while smoking a lit cigarette back home.

We find a dark, covered spot outside near the curb, and this is the first time Brandi and I are alone. There are no barriers or filters of environment or other people; it's just us —brother and sister.

We've had a few drinks—more than I'm used to and more than I'm comfortable with—and I decide to take a cigarette. Good, honest conversations come with drinking, but you have to really enjoy the company to abandon your spot at the bar and risk the elements outside to share a smoke. I take this as a sign of respect, and I imagine that I am a pilgrim toking with a native as an unsteady peace offering.

"I'm really happy you're here," she says to me.

"I'm glad I am too," I respond, exhaling the smoke calmly.

It's true. I am happy I am here, especially now, talking to Brandi. This is as exposed as we both have been with each other since—well, our whole lives. I think about how we were able to skip all that childhood bullshit, like sharing a bathroom and fighting over a parent's lap. It's as though we were able to meet free of expectations and past predictability.

The booze helps any emotional roadblocks, and puffing on our cigarettes gives us that extra pause to really think through our responses. I am learning a lot about her and my father. She seems to have a better grasp of who my father was, and I appreciate the unfiltered interaction. I know that whatever went on between me and my father was fucked up, but it's nice to have validation.

"I never could forgive him for asking you for money," she says. "It took a long time before I could speak to him after that."

"At least you spoke to him after that. I never got the chance to."

"It wasn't your responsibility to. He should have fixed it, but he just didn't know how."

I didn't know what to say. I want to accept some responsibility because it takes two people to make a relationship. I could have tried more. I could have reached out at any time and really had closure while he was alive.

"Neither did I," I say.

Brandi wipes a tear away and puts out her cigarette. "Enough with this," she says. "Let's go to The Lane."

We round up the herd and make our way a few doors down to The Lane Bar. Judging by the yelling and laughing, I can already tell this place has been around for a while. It's a dilapidated structure sandwiched between a more modern bar called The Stockman and a vacant copper outlet that smells like wet timber and gravel. Our posse squeezes in, and we're lucky to find an open section at the bar. Again, I see a "Firearms Welcome" sign at the back of the bar next to the top-shelf Wild Turkey whiskey.

"What will you have?" the young bartender asks.

"Shots!" says Brandi.

I feel a brush against my leg and look down to see a small, three-legged chihuahua sniffing my foot.

"Ummmm, does anyone else see a three-legged chihuahua sniffing my foot?" I inquire to my party.

"Oh yeah, he comes and goes," says the bartender as she pours a bright yellow mixture into five shot glasses.

"Is that why firearms are welcome?" I joke. "For the vicious three-legged chihuahuas?"

"No, it's actually because we get bears in here from time to time, smart-ass," she says, annoyed.

"What, you don't have many bears in Maryland?" Brandi asks.

"We do, but it's more of the kind that would meet Steven for a drink at Bar 47."

I'm fucking hilarious.

We grab our shots and hold them up, waiting for someone to say something grandiose and poignant—a few column words about the man we all lost and the opportunity we now have to start a new life with each other. Perhaps a quote from Frost or Hemingway.

"Let's get fucked up!" Brandi yells as we clink our glasses and toast to a night of new beginnings.

Brooke and Brandi head off toward the bathroom. I follow them with my eyes as if I'm instinctively trying to be a protective big brother. The truth is they're more than capable of taking care of themselves, and I'm proud they grew up to be strong. As they turn the corner, I see them go into another room in the bar. It's crowded, and a congregation of people is surrounding a stage where a man and a woman are singing a duet.

"Do you sing?" Bryan asks.

"Only in the shower," I reply.

Bryan smiles, and we talk more about what life is like for both of us in very different parts of the country. We laugh and bond over silly things and silly people we know, and I feel like we've known each other forever. Cal joins us but seems distracted as he sings whatever karaoke song is playing now at The Lane Bar's $2 Beer and Talent Night.

Cal looks at me and sings the chorus three inches from my face. He pauses like he's waiting for me to join in or finish the crescendo. He looks perplexed.

"You do know this song, right?"

"Sorry, I do not."

"Did you hear that, Bryan?" Cal yells. "Garth doesn't know this song!"

"You're kidding, right?" Bryan asks, his eyes in disbelief.

"We don't listen to much country music where I'm from," I say, suddenly shameful.

Brooke and Brandi return. They're both smiling and holding a slip of paper. They give it to Bryan, and he acknowledges the message with a nod of his head.

"Is that the one you'll sing?" Brandi asks proudly.

"Sure thing," he says, "but I doubt Garth will know it." He's fucking hilarious.

Bryan waits his turn to sing calmly, and Brandi looks super excited.

"Bryan's got an amazing voice," she tells me. "And how the fuck do you not know any of these songs?"

Bryan's number is up next, and he waves his slip of paper to the crowd as he makes his way to the stage. I'm too far away, and the bass is too high for me to make out what he's saying, but the crowd seems to know, and they give him a big cheer.

Of course, I have no fucking clue what song it is, but I'm surprised such a voice is coming from a man who ropes cattle and does real-man shit for a living. It's not feminine but sounds practiced and refined, and I wonder if Bryan ever had bigger ambitions to leave Montana and go to Nashville.

The crowd sings along and gathers around Bryan like he's Luke Brooks or Garth Bryant, and I look over to see how happy Brandi is. I think about our places in this life and the events that lead us to the people we love.

CHAPTER

Eighteen

SUGAR AND SPICE

Sex addicts must have it rough. I may have my crosses to bear, but I can't imagine the detox you have to go through to quit something that feels so naturally good and is vital to sustaining our existence. Unlike manmade addictions like booze and gambling, sex and food addicts are biologically ingrained to need what they crave in order to survive. I admire people who are brave enough to admit these addictions and have the willpower to quit. Saying "no thank you" to every kind of taco must be a horrible existence.

I don't think I have a sex addiction. I probably did at one point, but age, kids, and a poor Wi-Fi connection in my basement have whittled me down to an altar-boy-less priest. I can show up for mass, but I'm all talk. I do know that I have a relationship addiction, and that is just as hard to beat.

Relying on a relationship to define yourself is tricky and comes with a whole lot of problems. For me, it's a defining tragic flaw that puts all my emotional and physical eggs in one basket.

I lost my virginity at sixteen to a girl on a trampoline,

which set a high expectation for every woman since. She was a dramatic-arts girl who loved to dress in black and thought it was cool to defy her privilege by keeping her bedroom free of furniture. She literally had nothing in her room except tape outlines of friends on the floor, laid out in strange poses. It was like *CSI: EMO*, and it made sense that we had quick, awkward love on a fucking bouncy toy. But the sex didn't really keep me coming back. It was just being a "boyfriend." That title gave me some sort of definition, and I craved holding her hand and making her mix-tapes. Christ, I'm such a girl.

Since then, and until recently, women have been more of a distraction and a means of not being alone. It's having a partner for accountability and a sense of belonging. A lot of my friends from high school went on to marry their boyfriend or girlfriend right after graduation. Some made it, and some didn't, but it's an interesting quality that we brats share in comparison to peers who had a more traditional childhood. I think it's finding a home in something that is as mobile as you are, and in someone who understands the fleeting moment and fears being uprooted at any time.

My father never left Montana, but that didn't stop him from roaming different pastures. My mother often alluded to his adultery and spoke indignantly about him as a "son of a bitch." She never gave any details about his affairs, but he always seemed to have a woman in reserve.

I don't know the truth about what really happened when they split up and I was taken away, but it was done secretly and quickly while my father was away on some fishing trip. I was told by my mother that I was flown out of a dirt road in Montana as a baby on her brother's plane, under cover of night. I never questioned the validity of this story because I had no reason to, and it sounded so badass. That story, true or not, always made me feel special.

Regardless of what my backstory was, my father obviously had his issues with women. His sister told me stories of his relationship with his own mother and how his status as the only boy set him on a higher pedestal than his sisters. He was set up to be special, and maybe that placed the bar too high for any woman to reach.

He was married four times, with God knows how many affairs in between. His second wife—Brooke and Brandi's mom, Connie—came shortly after my mother. I remember Connie as being very rigid and stern. A true Montana woman who didn't have time to barter or negotiate because there was always something more urgent to do that pertained to survival. I was too young to appreciate her candidness, but now, knowing more about her relationship with my father, I understand why she was apprehensive of any male whose nomenclature was "MacKay."

My father divorced Connie after a few years and moved on to a woman named Nancy. What I know of Nancy has been passed down through stories from my sisters and Katie. Apparently, she was a disaster of a woman who tried to shape Brooke, Brandi, and my father into a Bible Belt representation of a modern family. Looking at pictures of their wedding, I can feel the tension, and I sympathize with my sisters' discomfort in their button-down blouses and linen skirts. Boy, am I glad I missed that one.

Again, my father left and moved on to Katie. I wish I could ask him why he kept moving. Was it a lack of physical attraction, or did he just get bored? I think about my own inclination to move on and how it's represented more in locations and experiences than in women. The more I learn about my father's relationships, the more I see that he had issues with women his whole life. Wives, girlfriends, daughters, and sisters all had trouble with him, and they had to put their relationships on hold to maintain their sanity and hold on to any shred of love they had for him.

The introspection of my father's toxicity over a long piss is short-lived as I walk back to our segregated seats in a new bar.

"Guess who I just saw?" Brandi says in a panic as she comes back from smoking another cigarette.

"Who?" Brooke says.

"Motherfucking Sugar!" Brandi replies like a tween getting a first-hand glimpse of Taylor Swift.

"Nooooooo!" Brooke says, as both girls' mouths hang agape and they huddle to talk about their next play.

The men are silent and confused as Brooke and Brandi look at each other in amazement.

"Holy fuck," Brandi shouts. "I bet she's here for the All-Years Reunion!"

I bite. "Who's Sugar?"

"Your mom never told you about Sugar?" Brooke asks. "Sugar dated Dad before he married your mom. One night they got into an argument at a dance, and your mom threw a drink in Sugar's face!"

"Shit," I mutter. "I must speak to this… Sugar!"

We stumble and stagger drunkenly down the one-road town, searching for the mythical figure known as Sugar. We peek into bar after bar until we spot a coven of old, familiar drunks encircling a bright, tight-skinned glow at the Lane Bar. And there, in all her Lululemon luminosity, is Sugar.

Like me, Sugar looks out of place in her tight white athletic bra. The only thing clinging more desperately to her altered 34DD tits is her younger male companion at the spry age of sixty. His name is David—or Davey—and he's wearing an Affliction T-shirt and smells like lemongrass and dirt. This guy's a bigger poser than I am…

I shuffle toward the bar, and I feel like, to an observer, I look like one of the horny old men vying to "taste some Sugar." I feel their jealous gaze and hear my sisters laughing at the awkward attempt I'm making to have my audience with the plastic princess.

I make my way to Sugar, and she is oddly bent back at the edge of the bar like a Picasso trying to be a Hopper. Her big lips are as bulbous and flashy as the boomer boners that surround her. I hesitate, trying to think about what I want to say, and that hesitancy lasts just long enough for Brandi to yell, "Are you fucking Sugar!?"

"Yes, I am!" she replies with pride.

"You knew our dad… Doug MacKay," Brandi states, more as a question.

"Oh yes, I do!" Sugar says. "How is he doing?"

"He died," Brandi says. "We're his kids, and we're here to lay his ashes tomorrow."

"Oh, I'm so sorry," she says while sipping her fruity cocktail. "He was a good, good man. So, you're his daughter?"

"I am." Brandi turns to me and Brooke and says, "And this is his other daughter, Brooke, and his son, Garth."

Sugar and I share a moment's glance, and she looks away to find her cigarettes. "I didn't know that he had so many kids. We haven't spoken in some time."

I hope she's lying, embarrassed to share memories in front of Davey—or David—but I want to know more about her and whatever bizarre relationship she had with my father. She takes a long drag and looks at Dave, or David, and strokes his hair. She's disengaging, obviously uncomfortable, but I need to know one thing.

"Is it true that my mother threw a drink in your face?" I blurt out like a Tourette's patient.

"What?!" she laughs. "Who is your mother?"

"Latricia Ludwick."

"I don't know her," she quickly responds.

It's exactly what I would say if someone asked me about a drink thrown in my face fifty years ago. Sugar turns around and finishes her drink. David—Davey, David—puts his arm around her waist and whispers something in her ear. She laughs, and I want to throw a drink in her face.

CHAPTER

Nineteen

DEPENDANCE DAY

ornings in Montana are very different from back home. I'm accustomed to waking up to calendar invitations and routine goings-on. Getting the kids up for school, packing lunches, and tying shoes. If it's a weekend or holiday, I can pretty much assume I am going to be told where and when to be by my wife. Our existence in suburbia is dictated by playdates, birthday parties, and our daily runs to Target.

All of which, I may add, have nothing to do with me or what my wife wants to do.

Yep, when it comes to time off, I have all of the control and decision-making influence of a toddler.

It's interesting how much the family dynamic has changed over the last few decades leading to today, and even well-rested, I am thinking about my family back east. Like the wise prophet Tom Keifer from Cinderella once wrote, "You don't know what you've got till it's gone." I find myself missing the fast-paced, scheduled hassle of my real life.

I'm trying to be present, and maybe that's why I'm

fixating on the wild comforts of home. Even though I think I have found a good groove here in the unpredictability of this journey, I am thinking of home.

It's 7:21 a.m. back east. This is the prime time that my ball-busting, cock-blocking son would barge into our bedroom and interrupt my feeble attempts at morning sex. He would be asking for high-fructose, frosted cereal, and I would be negotiating him down to something less synthetic. The negotiations would start civilized but would soon turn hostile as he rejects my final proposal of toaster-oven waffles and half a cup of sugar-free maple syrup.

His sisters (and allies) would then awaken and converge at the foot of the door, blankets and tenacity in arms, to assist in a tyrannical revolution and attempted coup of Sunday morning. Not just any Sunday morning, however—it's Independence Day.

The White Sulphur Springs Fourth of July Parade is about to begin. I haven't heard much from my sisters or Stacy yet, and I am trying to be more mindful about how this day, in particular, may be affecting them. Today is less about celebrating our collective freedoms as a nation; it's about facing what cages us as heirs to a broken family. Maybe it's fate that spreading his ashes and letting go is today, or maybe, just like anything else in his life, it's a series of happenstance and intrusive timing. Maybe I'm just being cynical, but even now it seems like I am the one being proactive.

I walk out of the hotel door into cool winds and gray skies. It's overcast, and I feel elated that I may actually be physically comfortable today—even though I have no fucking idea how I feel.

What am I really supposed to do today? Aside from never going to a funeral or memorial, I have no idea what my role is. Why am I even here? I don't really know these people or my father. I have been so invested in the moment-to-moment bullshit that I haven't thought about the weight of today. Fuck. I feel like a fluffer in a porn movie who is just there to sustain the mood until the real actors come in.

Even the logistics of spreading ashes are weird, but I understand why people do it. Hell, I told my kids that I want to be cremated too, but my reasons are more about not being a burden. I can't stand the thought of me in the ground with flowers and tears adorning my bed years after I'm gone. What a horrible, selfish routine to push on my loved ones. Even in death, I want to be pathetically accommodating.

I guess for my father, being spread on the mountains where he was raised, loved, and protected makes sense. I can't fault a person for wanting to stay home. Maybe it's the interlopers whose pale white asses are spread in the Caribbean because they caught a marlin once on a business trip 50 years ago. Those are the assholes.

Brooke is sitting with Cal, Jordan, and Katie across from the town hall, near the horse that is hinged with creaking copper bones in the steady gusts of wind. The old sculpture gives me pause the closer I get, and I identify with its unspoken mantra of simply following the nature of things. I see Brooke's thin smile and realize that this place, this time, is their home—and more importantly, their rules.

Brooke is bundled up in a sweatshirt I brought her from home, and whether she knows it or not, that makes me feel more included. I ask how she's feeling, and she looks sad.

"I'm okay… considering."

"Yeah, I bet," I say. "It's a big day."

I sit next to her, say good morning, and hug the rest of the family. I try to keep my eye contact and talking to a minimum without seeming like an unsympathetic asshole. It's hard to gauge what each person is feeling, and it's exhausting to keep up with the dynamics and levels of sorrow and grief.

Brooke is obviously torn up. She is staring across the street as if she's waiting for someone else to emerge from the motel. Katie and Laura are talking to each other, and I hear them laughing as the cars assemble for the parade in the lot behind the courthouse. Cal and Jordan are watching the horses lining up and anticipating the best spot to get the most candy. It's hard to read their emotions, but I imagine they are just trying to be present for Brooke.

There is no sign of Brandi yet. After last night, I am eager to see her. Our interaction over Camel and Bud Lights was cathartic and made me appreciate my sisters and their journeys. For the first time in my life, I feel a brotherly pride, and I accept that I am capable of letting more people in.

Across from us is the hospital. The orderlies wheel out the residents, who have a mean age of about 102. There are no new mothers and fathers, no daredevils with ATV injuries, and no cowboys with gonorrhea. They are all gray and dying, but at least they have prime seats.

Brandi and Bryan walk up from the cabins minutes before the parade starts. Brandi looks exhausted, and Bryan compliments her with a beaming smile and an optimistic outlook for the day.

We greet each other with smiles, and Brooke asks how she is doing.

"I'm okay," Brandi says while shaking her metal coffee tumbler. "Want some Rumchata?"

I'm both grateful and bothered that she wasn't talking to me. Of course, I want a numbing agent. This day is awkward as hell, and we haven't even gotten to the crowning of "Ms. White Sulphur Springs" yet. But looking across at the walking dead, I contend that my reluctant sobriety, at least for the next few hours, is paramount for my personal growth.

"Yes, please!" Brooke says as she eagerly grabs the hair of the dog.

They stand farther away from me and talk privately for a few moments as they share words and sips. Part of me—the codependent part—wants to know and be a part of their conversation. But like the old metal horse, the western breeze is keeping me sustained where I am.

Bryan comes over to me and reaches out his hand as I reach out my arms for a hug. Jesus, I am an awkward goon. I look like a desperate girlfriend trying to make amends after a one-night stand. I mistake his infectious positivity for personal affection, and now we have to do that awkward hug/handshake hybrid you see losers do at the Super Bowl. Brandi dries her eyes and comes over to me and gives me a hug. She rubs my back, and the small circles against my skin tell me, "It will all be fine."

The smell of sulphur dissipates, and the new scent of manure creeps in as the parade begins. Horses and ponies, and Fords and Chevys, break the silence on the concrete wall we claim. The local fire truck crawls by and throws out candy as Bar 47 represents itself with a makeshift float in the bed of an F-150. The barmaids and bus boys dress up like their old-timey compadres, complete with bow ties and garter belts.

A surprisingly elaborate float with yoga and Peloton cyclists rolls by, with modern branding and women who look like they are from back home. I haven't seen a pair of black yoga pants and Botox-filled cheekbones in almost a week, so I clap extra hard and wonder how the hell I missed this place.

The kids dart into the street and grab candy. It's mostly Tootsie Rolls, which I will never concede as "candy," but rather a dark, semi-sweet sludge that coats your throat until you hack thick spit for the next two hours. Occasionally, there is a rogue Rolo or hidden 100 Grand that's uncovered, but there seems to be a deliberate lack of Hershey's or Reese's. This all seems very anti-American to me, especially today.

When the last car rolls by, I am still trying not to gawk at the mayor's horse's ginormous red cock as the elders are rolled back into their dormant state, the shit is shoveled off the street, and the residents of Bar 47 are dropped off to resume business as usual. Then the entire town disperses. Unlike most parades I have been to back home, the town continues to celebrate in the streets, shops, and bars. Back home, the heat and crowds are at max capacity, and most parents' resilience has been strained as they retreat back to their air-conditioned Escalades.

I wonder if it's safe and acceptable to take in the town's joy on a day that is supposed to be sedated and melancholy. I look over at the copper horse as the wind steers his head in an up-and-down motion.

That seems like a yes to me.

Unspoken, we all make our way to Bar 47, our common space where we all seem most comfortable. It's a large space for large conversations, and we all have a lot to talk about. I just hope I'm not the one doing all the talking.

"Garth?!… Garth, is that you?"

I am pinned between Brooke and Brandi with my back toward the door. I glance back and see two older ladies, dressed very nicely and conservatively, accompanied by an older, gray-haired, tan gentleman in nice khakis and a polo shirt.

Before I see their eyes, I see the sunlight glistening off the tears on their faces. The shorter, darker one pulls me up by the face and looks soulfully into my eyes.

"I am your Aunt Carol," she says, her warm hands on my scruffy cheeks. "My God, you look just like your father."

For the first time, I feel a welling inside that is way down deep. It's a strange feeling when someone you don't know tells you that you look like someone you don't know. It questions your reality and general existence. It's overwhelming to be seen in a way that you never knew—or could even contemplate. It's like being born again.

I am fighting tears, not because I don't want to let go, but because I don't know how. There is a block that I have, and it's like a dam holding back years of pain, questions, and anger. I know that someday, sometime, it's going to break, and the flood will be destructive. I'm sure as hell not doing it now around bison burgers and IPAs.

Aunt Elaine and her husband, Casey, follow suit, and we all sit down to talk about the past and prepare for the present. Moments later, Stacy comes in from Manhattan, and again I feel like I have another person to lean on. It looks like the gang is all here.

I look across the long oak table and see a group of people talking to each other, sharing food, drinks, common existences, and predisposed patterns, and at the end of that long hearth is me. I am taking questions and filtering my responses so as not to upset anyone. I share my memories at the table like an appetizer. Questions like "What do you remember about your father?" and "Where did your mother take you after she left Montana?" are dips in the communicative jelly, and I am happy to appease everyone.

I feel like I am a small part of these people, and even if it's the small, dark, hollow knot, it's still good to be part of the table.

The sun sits high above Main Street, and the sound and smell of engines really punctuate what it means to be an American. The town is filled with chatter and laughs, and the hues feel ripped and desaturated, like an old vintage film reel. It's an episode of *Mayberry* directed by Michael Bay, with a live performance from Trace Adkins sponsored by Chevy Trucks. Children run loose throughout the streets as the parents drink outside, engaging with neighbors and wanderers like me.

There is no timeline for the day per se, but I think we all feel the weight of what needs to be done. For my newly found aunts, I think they just want closure. My father has been in a handmade, decoratively bedazzled Quaker Oatmeal container for over a year, and I imagine there is some relief in letting him out. I sense that for Katie and my sisters, it's the opposite. I think they want him to remain a part of their lives, and that putting him to rest means never seeing him again. For me, I just feel like it needs to be done. It's been a persistent pull to complete this, and I still don't know if that's a normal feeling.

Everyone finishes their lunch and drinks, and we all feel the courage and motivation to start our journey up the mountain. It's going to be a long way up to where my father wanted to be set free. It's a place he liked to go when patrolling the forest and a place everyone associates with his peace and happiness. It's a spot where you have to walk carefully not to upset the balance of things. It's raw and savage and quiet, and maybe that's why my father liked it here.

We load into Cal's four-wheel-drive truck, followed by Katie and Laura in a Civic hatchback. The road to the mountain pass is about ten miles out of town, and it's as far west as I've been in Montana so far. The one-lane highway is surrounded by old barns and bright green pastures. Linens hang outside the occasional cabin nestled high on ridges, and the smell of pine and sulphur seeps through my veins.

We pass several areas with U.S. Forest Service signs and warnings, mostly about bears, until we come to a secluded gravel turn that is overrun with weeds and broken wooden beams. Cal doesn't slow down much as we slide and careen along the unstable road and barrel down the path, shooting dirt behind us and signaling our location to the car behind. The road narrows and slowly becomes more enveloped by its natural state. We pull aside and wait for the Civic to climb to where we are situated. I see a plume of dust rise down the road, and we get out to get our bearings. The girls point and argue as the men confirm the best direction to go.

The route up is rocky and dangerous, and it's decided that Katie and Laura won't be able to go much farther on foot. There is a strange, unspoken power struggle between my father's wife and daughters over where exactly the ashes are to be spread, but Brandi's perseverance and unbending will decide that we venture as deep as we can—with or without Katie.

Brandi holds on to the ashes as Cal reaches deep into the bed of the dusty truck. Among live bait and stains of God knows what else, an aged Igloo cooler is filled with long-necks of Coors Light, and each of us takes one silently. Bryan walks a few feet ahead and surveys the path as Cal waves to the lagging car far behind. The sky grows darker, and a faint rumble of thunder echoes through the valley.

"Yep, that's Dad all right," says Brooke, as Brandi's eyes widen and glaze over with tears. The two share an embrace and sob quietly as the men lean in to comfort them. Stacy and I look at each other as observers, more or less detached from the jolt of sentiment that was just shared.

I wish I could feel the impact of what they are feeling—the embrace of something bigger and the certainty of hearing something meant just for me. Even if I had been close to my father, I don't think I have that free-range sentimental quality that can emote a response to something so spiritually benign. It strikes me that they are in tune with something larger than I am, and I feel empty.

I've been a son, father, husband, and friend and have never allowed myself to feel loss and grief at that level. I was never certain about my place or relationship with death and letting go. I cling to happiness, like roots entangled deep in the earth. My unease and hesitancy to experience sadness have led me to a life of dependency.

RULE: DON'T FEEL BAD

Another roll of thunder crashes closer, and my sisters cry harder and hold each other tighter. When each electrified impulse charges the air, I think back to times when I ran for cover. My best friend died of leukemia when we were twenty-two. I never went to the funeral. My grandfather, who was the only male role model I had until Pops, died a few years ago, and I never went to his funeral. I turn the page on sad stories, and I make up better ones. I pretend things are better, people are kinder, and problems are softer in an effort to stay happy. When I can't bend the world to my sunny will, I escape through alcohol, depression, and distortion. At my lowest, I wanted a quick way out. The work to get "better" seemed intimidating, and I surrendered to being beyond repair. I wasn't happy, and I couldn't create a space that allowed me to be free of pain. Now here I am on this mountain, surrounded by grief and sadness in their rawest, most intimate form—and I can't run. Even if I could, this is still his mountain.

Before I can invest more time in my thoughts, Katie and Laura arrive, and we make the unanimous plan to hike up as far as we can with the older ladies, split the ashes there, and drive onward to the spot my father wanted.

We embark slowly up the side of the mountain, and I find that I can escape feeling bad by staring at my feet, looking for snakes and avoiding bear shit. Brooke and Brandi are in front, rotating holding their beers, the ashes, and each other. I see their awkward shifting and walk softer so they forget I'm there.

"Garth, want to hold Dad?" Brandi says.

I've never held my father. I don't remember him holding me. Now I have to hold him?

"Sure," I say. "There's a first time for everything."

Twenty

RITE OF PASSAGE

Y ou don't know how much ashes weigh until you've trekked them up a rocky mountain path in Montana on a hot July afternoon. It's deceptively heavy for something that occupies so little space, and I can't help comparing it to the ruck marches from the military. I was much younger then and had the benefit of someone yelling in my ear, calling me a "faggot" if I faltered for even a second.

This is much more serene. I'm pushed onward by older women nipping at my heels. I also feel my age as my drooping testicles steadily stick to the back of my knee.

I stride alongside my sisters, who are walking quietly, and I feel the urge to say something stupid to lighten the mood. Instead, I return to the realization that I need to feel this. So I turn my attention back to my father.

He's really heavy. For something that is basically just a fraction heavier than air, it has a surprising substance. I cradle it—him—the ashes in my arms, and it feels like I'm carrying a child. I stay with that analogy, trying not only to feel the weight in my arms, but the weight in my heart.

This isn't the assertive sadness everyone else feels at losing something, nor is it the passive anger over something being taken away. It's a weight that actually feels lighter with each step, as I experience the only real connection I have ever had with my father. It's an unedited, unbiased love for someone who has never left me. It's the kind of love you'd feel for a donor's family after waking up with a new heart, or for the stranger who blew air into your lungs when you were drowning.

I look down at the handmade urn and appreciate its earnest decoration. It's adorned with photographs of my father through the years—from a young man with light in his eyes to the end, where he looks ready to walk into the ocean. I see his stages mirrored in my own. I see the divergence in our paths, and the conscious decision I've made not to disappear.

I notice his law enforcement badges glued to the container and understand what he valued—and how losing that identity must have sent him spiraling. I recognize his handwriting on the strips of paper he left for Katie when he knew the end was near. The sentiment is matter-of-fact, written in a voice that feels foreign to me.

I realize this vessel is filled with what others believed mattered most to him. I'm not here—and that's okay. I don't feel slighted or abandoned. I don't feel angry or hurt. Beyond our shared blue eyes, what we truly had in common was a dependence on finding happiness by whatever means necessary. And through circumstances both within and beyond our control, we decided that being at peace with ourselves could not coexist with each other.

The sky grows darker, and the wind picks up. We reach a clearing on the trail where Katie stops, resting and struggling to catch her breath. She surrenders to her age and abilities and decides she's gone far enough. I hand the ashes back to Brandi, and she carefully pours a lidful into the container and passes it to Katie.

My epiphany gives way to Katie's eulogy. She speaks sweetly about my father, crying as she talks from the heart, and I feel grateful that he found someone who could love him despite his lifelong struggles and flaws. Whether it was a genuine storybook love, a lack of options, or simple convenience, it was something that brought her happiness. I like to think that when he took his last breath, he felt that too.

Katie releases the ashes, and they pour steadily back to the earth. The spectacle of spreading ashes had always seemed much grander in my imagination, and I wonder if she's disappointed by my father's final act of grandeur.

"Why don't you rest here?" Brooke says to Katie. "We're going to go to the top."

I feel bad that Katie will spend the next hour alone on the side of the mountain. I also briefly wonder if she'll be eaten by bears or sasquatches. Cal leaves a few beers with her, and the rest of us continue upward.

About a half mile later, we reach another clearing. It's a peaceful stretch of land surrounded by old fence posts and clumps of dried tracks left by recreational vehicles. The road ends here and opens onto a landscape that briefly deceives you into thinking you've reached the pinnacle—until you notice the sister mountains jutting up from the Rockies beyond it.

Stacy always told me that I'm part of this place, that Montana is in my blood. I never really knew what she meant. I chalked it up to her theatrical background—her instinct to turn everything into a good story. But standing here now, I think I finally understand. On this uncommon pass, with these common people, I feel the pull to belong and a sense of history. I don't know if I'm lost in the serenity or distracted by thoughts of death, but I feel like I belong here.

One by one, we take turns pouring our share of ashes into the lid and casting them into the wind. Brooke goes first. Her eulogy is tearful, brief, and final.

"We made it, Dad," she says, sweeping her hand across the horizon as she releases the ashes into the open plain.

Brandi is less forthcoming with words. She fights back her tears, holding her portion of our father with less attachment and more urgency to be done. She throws the remains high into the air like a magician performing a final trick, then beats the empty canister against her leg to shake loose every last grain.

Stacy, Brian, and Cal each step up, and we watch one another in moments that are raw and unguarded. Stacy is mindful. She shares thoughts of her favorite uncle and gently spreads her share like a lonely old woman feeding pigeons. Cal steps forward silently, takes his turn, raises a beer, and toasts the wind. Brian shares brief, impactful memories of my father. He says he wishes he'd known him longer, and I feel ashamed that he may have known him better than I did.

Brooke kneels and pours a lidful of my father's ashes, then hands it to me. I forget—until that moment—that I have a part in this. I'm caught off guard and unprepared, unsure what I'm supposed to say or what needs to be heard. I feel pressure to honor my father—as a conduit of my own life, as the glue that somehow kept us steady on this mountain. But I don't have the sentiment an only son is supposed to have, and I don't know how to summon anything but hollow words or fake promises about always carrying him with me.

Then I realize he never left.

He isn't the romanticized presence he is for everyone else here, but I feel our kinship in crisis—and the finality of letting each other go so we can start over. In that moment, I understand what he meant to me.

Douglas MacKay was the Big Bad Wolf, the scorpion on the frog's back, Mount Vesuvius. A natural, disastrous antagonist—exactly the kind every great story needs. His life was a peephole version of what mine could have been, maybe should have been. I think about how often I erupted, how many times I destroyed someone to move ahead, how seductive the world looks through the eyes of a predator.

I am finally able to define our relationship. After years of living and hours of therapy, it's clear. We were each other's bad guys—the person to whom we could assign blame and designate as the cause of all of our life's problems. Our relationship made for sad, drunken fodder with strangers and the foundation of codependent relationships meant to fill the missing gaps.

We were each other's boogeyman, but now that the sun is out, I can see that it is just a shapeless shadow cast on the wall, and everything is going to be fine.

I am holding the end story in my hands, and the ashes graze against the cardboard and dance with each gust of wind. Like my siblings, I have an opportunity to punctuate his history how I choose. Part of me—his part, maybe—wants to be cold and vindicate those he left in his wake: his sisters whom he took from, his daughters whose trust and promises he broke, his wives whom he drained and abandoned, and me, whom he never got to know.

I think about him at the foot of the ocean and me at the entrance of an autumn pass. He is walking in that cold, infinite space trying to find footing while I am huddled deep and alone, looking at the matte finish of a shotgun. He is full of despair and regret as the ocean envelopes him, and the press of the trigger against my thumb brings me peace.

The saltwater presses against his lips, and the cold barrel parts mine.

We are at this precipice together—Father and Son—and we both turn away and walk back to Montana.

I sift the ashes in my hand as a breeze bellows down the sister mountains to the north. I hold his remains in my hand and close my eyes. The breeze suddenly picks up and becomes a strong gust that hits against my back and sends chills down my spine.

"Let me go, Son," I hear my father saying.

I release the rest of my father with each current. It dissipates and blurs softly on the horizon, and my knees buckle.

It's over.

Twenty~One

SHINY THINGS

My father's generation is the last one to leave things behind. Not just self-doubt, unrealized dreams, and emotional affliction; I mean physical mementos. I'm thinking about what I can leave behind to my kids that will increase in monetary and emotional value when I die, and I can't think of anything of weighted substance.

That's sad. The only things that I use and am associated with are replaced by software updates or new technology from China. "…And to my son, I bequeath my rose gold iPhone 4 that I reluctantly took because I was too impulsive to wait until they got the matte black one in stock. Don't worry, I also left you my camouflage Otterbox case, so people won't think you're gay. To my daughters, I bestow upon you the digital license and passwords to every movie and streaming service that I have signed up for. Rewatch Bill Paxton's performance in *Aliens* and think fondly of me. And to my wife Jennifer, the most important person in my life, I leave you detailed instructions on how to reset the router, the HVAC filter sizes, and the garbage removal schedule on the refrigerator's whiteboard. I love you forever. P.S. Don't fuck any of my friends LOL."

We're all drained as we head back from the mountain, as our journeys are now complete, and we gather for an informal ceremony at the local recreation center. Like the town, this place is shrouded in history and looks like a mausoleum. It's wrapped in oak lumber and held together by pictures of Rotary Clubs and "Beware of Bears" flyers. There is no sign that we have an event scheduled here today, but it seems like the kind of place where you just show up.

Brandi had come here early to set up, and the tables that are scarred with bingo dotters are now transformed by homemade centerpieces and collages of my father. I look over the place and the people that are entering. I don't know any of the new wanderers, but after sharing condolences and stories, Katie and my sisters pass them by me, where I'm hiding by the coffee.

"Oh my God! You're Garth? Doug's son?" They seem disappointed, or maybe they thought I was a drunken vision of one of my father's benders. Either way, it's still strange to be associated with him, and the atmosphere becomes more catered to an AA meeting. The trips to the coffee machine veer toward different people and conversations, and I feel like I'm just a dream.

I sit with Brooke, Brandi, Cal, Bryan, Jordan, and Stacy, and the proceedings begin with an opening eulogy from Katie. Her voice cracks and gets disrupted by moments of loss and humor. She's less sad than when we were at the mountain, and I feel relieved that I don't have to console anyone by proxy of being the next man in line.

Bryan sets up his guitar and plays an acoustic anthem to my father. It's a beautiful rendition of some country song that I have never heard, but I get the sad feelings you're expected to get when hearing country at a funeral. Now there's a niche back home I should explore...

Old men and friends of my father step up and talk about

him as a great hero. A man of irrefutable strength and bravery who loved being in danger. I hear about his unnatural ability to read fire and determine its path. I imagine him as a real version of a fairy tale and think about how the other kids' faces would have looked at our Career Day presentation.

Like me, he had a desire to be looked at as an example of morality and a positive leader in his community. He was reverent in the tales, and I hope that I will someday be remembered as he was. Whether it was true or not.

As the last words were spoken and the crowd dispersed to their fried chicken and coleslaw platters, Katie pulls out a deep Ziploc bag. It is filled with clumps of metal and brass and is pulling under the strain. She empties it on the long table in front of her and fans out its contents with her feeble hands.

It's a trove of things my father used and cherished throughout his life. Among the contents are a pair of cuff links that his father gave him; his law enforcement pins and medals; and various pieces of jewelry.

Katie tells us all, friends and family, that my father would want us to have these things and to take what we want. I look at the bounty, and it slowly gets picked off, one shiny sentimental piece at a time. The gold Rolex is one of the first things to go. It's gestured to me to take, but I decline, knowing that it's probably a fake and that my father's debts and addictions would surely claim anything of real value. Instead, I watch what people want and silently judge them. Savages.

"I think your dad would have wanted you to have this," Stacy says as she holds out her hand. Inside is a heavy silver-toned mass that looks like a large locket found in an antique jewelry store. Stacy opens it. "It was your dad's compass. He took it with him all the time, and I think he would want you to have it."

I reluctantly take it from Stacy. Just being here feels like I pulled into someone else's driveway by mistake, and actually taking his property feels like trespassing. Sentiment, I guess, overpowers me, and I inspect the old compass. It feels like a prop, and now all of a sudden, I feel like this is all planned on purpose to get me to feel something. It's too cliché for my cynicism. Finding my direction. Point North. Follow your path. Blah blah blah, but I don't want to be rude. I hold it tight in my hand, trying to feel a connection, at least for Stacy's sake.

Then a small round glint signals to me from the heap. It's a thin silver charm that is no bigger than the diameter of a dime and probably similar in value. It's overturned a few times and overlooked as perhaps part of something bigger. To my eye, it's a flash of something spiritually meaningful, and I inspect it further. It's less shiny the closer I get, as the smudges and decay from decades of wear leave it dull and humble. I feel there is a brilliance beyond the modest façade and a lost meaning buried in the grit. I bring the charm closer and can barely decipher some text etched on the flat surface.

"10-17-74." My birthday.

This is the answer to why I came. Among the grand landscapes, large new family, weighted emotions, and high expectations, the key to everything was this small thing. The token of confirmation that I did exist and physical proof that he did know me. At some point in his life, he even loved me. Someone gave him this charm. Maybe it was a paternal passage from the heart of his father or my mother. Maybe it was a last-minute gift from a friend who was caught up in a giant blizzard or attacked by a bear. Fuck, maybe it was a secret gift from Sugar. In my mind, maybe it was a gift for him to record the first time he felt proud to be a father.

I cup it more gently in my hand and embrace it with care. I inspect the broken links that once held the chain around his neck. It could have easily been lost or tossed aside, but here it is. I wonder why he kept it all these years and if anyone took the time to look at it closer. I take the end of my shirt and polish it like rubbing your eyes in the morning to get a better view. I turn the charm around, and lighter than my birthday reads...

"World's Greatest Dad."

Maybe not, but we sure as hell are trying our best.

Twenty-Two

GUILT TRIP

I n 18A, the row ahead of me in 19B, an Indian couple is traveling with their kid. I have been lucky that it's not screaming, but my luck runs out as they change its diaper. If you can imagine what Indian food smells like, imagine what it smells like coming out of the asshole of a three-year-old at 30,000 feet above Ohio. This is the first time that I am thankful to be wearing a mask. What the fuck is wrong with people? There are clearly places in the bathroom to do this satanic ritual that don't involve half the plane having watery eyes.

Fucking assholes.

I told myself when I flew out of Bozeman today that I was going to be a better person. The fresh air and mountainous valleys that engulfed me for the last week inspired me to do better, but Sanje, or whatever the fuck his mom is calling him, is making me revert to my old patterns.

Maybe it's not Sanje. Maybe it's the text my mom sent me before the flight. It was a callous, insecure text that read: "I heard you were in Montana. Hope you find what you were looking for. Good luck in the future."

Find. Not Found. I'm irate.

Narcissists can't imagine themselves being left out of life-changing self-discoveries and mask their anger with finality. She has no desire for me to have peace and closure at the expense of her failures and insecurities. She will never understand what this trip represents and the hell I had to go through to get on the plane.

She spent the best years of her life in Montana. She found love, she made a home, and she had a child here. I saw pictures of her smiling and eating wedding cake. I heard nice stories about her from people who could have easily told me the worst. I stood in fields where she chased friends and sat on wood-splintered benches where she ate ice cream on hot summer days.

She hates Montana but can't let it go. No matter how bad he was or wasn't, she never dealt with the loss of that relationship, and I remind her of that pain. I have to remind myself that since he is truly gone, I am the source of her unhappiness. It's so hard to love someone that can't love you back, and I must make peace with that. I wish she could forget about this place and focus on something good. I learned that I will never know the truth of their pain and past, but I love Montana.

I love Montana the same way I love her and my father. The same way I love Pops and my wife and all of my children. I love that it's a place where love can exist in the past and ripple into the future. I love thinking there was a place where my mother taught me to walk on a green shag carpet. I love thinking that my father's addictions weren't because he felt trapped by me, but because he was trapped by himself.

I love to think of them finding each other in a town where people go to get lost. I love thinking of the spark that led to their first kiss and the giddiness they must have felt during a first dance. I love that my mom was a badass and threw a drink in the face of a woman named Sugar for hitting on my dad because that's what Jenny would do.

I love to think about them making plans with the best of intentions and the heartbreak they must have felt when those intentions fell apart. I love to think that my mom's only option was to leave and take me with her. I want to be worthy of a good life and have a mother that fought hard to keep me safe. I love to think about a father missing a son and riddled with the anger of abandonment and sadness of loss. I want to be a father who would grieve for the loss of a child and go to every length to find them.

On the day we scattered Douglas Harlan MacKay's ashes, I was finally able to let go. As the white powder left my hands and got lost in the clouds of the big sky, I felt free. I didn't feel the pull between tradition and presence that made me question who I am and where I came from.

I wanted this journey to be a symbolic end. Not just by returning a man's ashes to the earth, but to find closure and make sense of the demons that follow me. This trip is more than miles; it's years. It's validation of things I know, answers to questions I had, and a breath of new life to one I wanted to smother.

Nicole tells me that I should use this time to write a journal and reflect on my thoughts. She thinks it's a valuable tool to express my feelings and address issues as they happen. It's also supposed to be a way to say goodbye to negativity by acknowledging your pain on paper and cathartically releasing it off your burdened soul. I'm trying to be more receptive to these things, but it's still difficult to leave old rules and start anew.

I should just let my mother's snide comment go and focus on the positive aspects of the trip. I met new family members that want to see me happy. I learned about things that made me know how I am and what I can do to be better. I grew deeper in love with my family after seeing what neglect can do. So, why should I fucking care?

I sit back deep into my coach seat and take a deep, insufferable breath. I tense up my arms once again to feel what physical discomfort means and then relax them to feel the power I release at will. I close my eyes and think about how this one text can trigger me back to my old patterns so quickly. I wanted to use this time to journal and take mental snapshots of what my psyche is feeling so I can refer to them much later after the high of the trip wears off.

But no. She ruined that. Again.

I look at the empty pages of my journal as Sanje winds down and his sobs are muzzled by my own heavy head. I start by writing about where I'm at physically and what I'm feeling emotionally, and all I can come up with is four BIG letters carved deep with graphite.

F.U.C.K.

I regress for a moment and think, "It's not supposed to be like this," "Be a man," "Leave the past in the past," and "What's the point? We're all going to die."

Then, I decide to change the present narrative and look to the future. I smile and start to write.

"New Rules."

Epilogue
NEW RULES

It's 6:30 am and the warming sun is starting to rise out of my front window. The glint against the pane shows the messy fingerprints of my kids, and it's a testament to their own curiosities and journeys. I pour a cup of coffee and sit down with my thoughts, and it's like meeting an old friend. One thing that I don't ever want to change is waking up early.

It's been almost three months since I have been back from Montana, and the emotional dust has settled. My father's ashes are in an oak urn with me on the seventh shelf of my bookcase behind my writing table. It's a blissful and cautionary reminder that he's here - watching over me. I feel like I've been given a second chance to make him proud as he watches me work over my shoulder.

Fall in Maryland is beautiful, and I can't imagine any other place I'd rather be. The frost creeps back in like an evening tide, and the leaves fall into each whispering of the wind. I'd like to go back to Montana during this time of year and see if I feel the same as I do now. Is it the time, the place, or is it me that's changed?

I've had a bit of a misstep in the last week. With school starting and the kids going back, my son and I have been triggering each other with homework and social expectations. I find myself wearing out easily with him, and I can feel myself disengaging and being pulled into old bad habits.

I decided to return to journaling, so I break out the notebook I used in Montana. I haven't wanted to use it since I've been back because I thought I was cured. I opened it up to my last entry on July 6.

NEW RULES

IT *IS* SUPPOSED TO BE LIKE THIS

I've never been religious, and saying that I am an atheist sounds much too permanent. If there is a God, I'd like to be able to say I was on the fence about the whole thing and not just a petulant jerk who had a visceral disdain for something I didn't know or was exposed to. Saying that I'm agnostic also sounds like a cop-out, but I appreciate not taking something as important as faith at face value. Call it destiny or the intervention of a higher power, but I am starting to be less cynical about the timing of life events and considering the possibility that things are as they should be. Maybe I wasn't supposed to know my father in the way that everyone else did. Maybe my father was supposed to be a mythos that was undeniably vacant so I could connect with Pop the way I had and be a better father to my own children. Maybe I'm not supposed to have a good relationship with my mother so I could surrender to my wife's support, see my sister's grief, and accept the value and strengths of the women in my life. But most importantly, maybe I had to see the listlessness in my mortality so that I could take the urgent steps to appreciate what I had in my wonderfully dysfunctional life.

BE OPEN TO CLOSURE

I suspect that change is difficult for most people, and the last year was my own testament to challenging old expectations and opening myself up to new experiences.

Before finding therapy, I had the wrong idea about closure. To me, leaving the past in the past was as simple as shutting a cabinet door. It was a conditioned response to things that needed to be done but shouldn't require any extra thought. Blocking lost memories and my reluctant ability to find answers was easier than getting on a plane and putting in the work to keep closing the door.

So, moving forward with the new me, I want to be better at peeking inside the things that make me sad, depressed, or anxious. For me, learning how to have a healthy relationship with the darkness makes me appreciate and acknowledge the good things I have in my life even more.

MEN ASK FOR HELP (STILL, NOT DIRECTIONS)

When I caught Covid a few months before I left, I was convinced that the secret to beating the virus was going to be overloading my immune system with hot toddies. I was shocked that my research came across little information or trial studies on how whiskey and lemons could obviously cure the coronavirus. After all, it cures most colds, sore muscles, and memories of sleeping with that lazy-eyed stripper with a fresh caesarean section scar. But I digress.

When I tested positive, I immediately went to the liquor cabinet, said goodbye to my family, and retreated to the basement where, in a few days, I would emerge victorious and immune forever. Sadly, it just made me dehydrated and probably hindered my overall recovery.

I spent the next few weeks moaning on the couch and almost being admitted to the hospital for COVID pneumonia.

Luckily, my wife and her family spent tons of time aiding in my recovery by finding speakeasy monoclonal antibody clinics, shady B-12 IV administrators, and daily well-wishes and doctor blogs. It's not an exaggeration to say I almost didn't make it. At one point, I actually think I did die for a few moments as I felt calm and peace that was like slipping into a warm bath.

Like my physical battle with COVID, my mental battle with depression wasn't going to be solved with half-assed research, toxic theories, or alcoholic dependence. It wasn't until I was at my lowest point that I felt the emotional weight I was carrying, and having support from my family and friends literally saved my life.

Now, I fucking love therapy. I get to talk to someone unbiased for an hour and can literally say whatever I want. There is no judgment or bias or hurt feelings afterward. A good therapist can be a sounding board for the problems in your life and offer viable, safe solutions to combat stress and anxiety.

Even when I wasn't actively asking for help, Jenny was always keeping an eye on me, and my reluctance to start therapy must have caused her a lot of undue stress. Being as codependent as we are, I take her cue when she senses my issues are returning and schedule a meeting with Nicole every now and then. Therapy is like taking a hot shower after working in the bitter cold all day. It's time to focus on cleaning the dirt off and taking the time to appreciate what self-care feels like.

DRUGS ARE AWESOME!

Fuck you, Nancy Reagan, I NEED my fix!

I'm still not entirely convinced that the small pills I take before bed and when I wake up actually work, but I have to trust the people close to me when they say, "Wow, you're not an insufferable asshole anymore!"Even though my sporadic "touch-up" therapy sessions come in handy for long-term stuff, the antidepressants and serotonin boost sure make the day better. Finding the right balance is a pain in the ass and can take some time, but the benefit of having the right dose is vital to keeping with the psychiatric plan.

I don't carry the stigma of "needing" medication to be functional. In fact, the more time I spend medicated, the more my doctor and I think I may actually be bipolar. That diagnosis is something I will have to make peace with and learn to adapt to, but having a good treatment plan and a relatable psychiatrist that works in tandem with my therapist has taught me to embrace the short- and long-term effects of the right medication.

STAY AWAY FROM THE SWEET STUFF

My time chasing Sugar from bar to bar made me realize that I was really chasing a false narrative. I was chasing the idea of what I wanted my father and mother to be. I wanted Sugar to have an unfiltered story about them that wasn't tainted with anger or resentment. I really thought Sugar was going to tell me the sweet story of two people who loved each other and had an amazing son that was going to do amazing things.

But she didn't even know that story, much less my story. I surmise that her validation would somehow have made me feel more validated and would have been another person that had access to the good parts of my father and the possessive nature of my mother.

Our interaction taught me to have confidence in what I know to be true and to be skeptical of things I want to be true. Part of my depression came from me wanting the world to be a certain way and not accepting the way things actually are. I still want to dream and hope for the best, but moving forward I don't want to deny the hard truths and get stuck in the cycle of wishful thinking.

I accept that there are things that I will never know about my father.

I will never know the man that my sisters know. The man who made them feel safe when the chill of Montana's winter boarded up their homes and the only heat came from him. I won't know that man who took pride in his work and community and honored his parents by showing up for supper every Sunday night. But, more importantly for me, I will never know the father who passed out on the sofa from drinking too much or the panic his family must have felt each time he called at midnight to ask for money to get out of trouble. I suppose to know him came at a price and that price was loving him at an arm's distance and never truly letting him in. It's possible, I think, that even if he was a constant in my life, I wouldn't have had the relationship I needed with him anyway.

BE A *GOOD* MAN

My sisters told me that once when my father was on patrol in the mountains, he came across a giant grizzly bear. Legend has it that the two-ton bear charged him with the ferocity of everything ancient and wild. His hot, fevered breath broke through the deep freezing as he trucked savagely toward my father. Calmly, my father brandished his

.45 and shot the creature between the eyes as he was in mid-leap. The bear died in the air and collapsed right at my father's courageous feet. So the story goes....

My father was a huge presence to competitors and wildlife, both off and on the field. His six-foot frame and hulking stance made him a massive and intimidating player in high school. From what I heard, he wasn't a funny man per se. Making people laugh wasn't something that was in his wheelhouse, and certainly, there were no tales of his hilariously legendary pranks or handed-down fart jokes. I spent a lot of time wondering what he would have thought of me as a man.

I'm not particularly big or competitively athletic. I never had one great story about how I stole the ball at the last second and scored the winning goal during the big game. My athletic accomplishments have always been personal and spiritual. I never wanted to be carried off a field in celebration when I could revel in cutting a minute off my personal 5K run time or holding that one yoga pose a few extra seconds. I'm not sure how my father would have reacted to my physical accomplishments when they couldn't be celebrated out loud by screaming fans or the local sports page.

Defining "what is a man" is something that I believe evolves with each passing year or milestone in a man's life. If you told me 20 years ago when I first became a father, that I would have to worry that I may have assigned them a gender without their consent, I would have told you to remove the tampon from your ass and kick rocks. The times are changing, and maybe I've become more lax than I thought I would.

Maybe it's the medication, or the mental breakdown, or the vasectomy, that made me appreciate the subtle context that makes me the man of the house.

When Jenny took my guns after my suicidal ideations, I felt the barren emptiness and shame of not being able to adequately protect my family. If someone broke in and I didn't have the means to protect them, it was my own fault. That was a hard pill to swallow, and I struggled deeply with not having the right tools to do what a man needs to do. I resented her in those moments for taking the last of my virility and reducing me to a soy latte-drinking sissy boy. It took me a long time to realize that what she did saved my life and that access to tools of destruction would have probably killed me—all in the name of "being a man."

Maybe it's the "new me," or my testosterone is extremely low, but I feel calmer and more comfortable in the fact that whatever wildlife the suburbs can throw at me, be it squirrel, raccoon, or solar panel solicitor, I can fend them off with intimidating signs and profanity.

I'M ROBIN

Dr. Fowler once told me that, at any time after starting my new meds, should I feel like a superhero, I should STOP IMMEDIATELY. Feeling invincible is a sign of a manic episode, and with those great highs come great lows.

My Batman analogy on how to fly made me realize that I embrace the archetype of being in change and in power too much. I felt the opposite in Montana. I didn't feel small, but I didn't feel like I had to solve every problem either. It was a nice balance of knowing and learning. I was conscious of the people and surroundings but not prepping for the bad to come in and cause havoc. I was more mindful in the passenger seat, and perhaps that is where peace and I should ride.

BREATHE IN AND DRIVE SLOW

The nomadic lifestyle that I was so accustomed to, defined myself as, and loved as a young man was slowly destroying me as I got older. The constant movement and shifts in my location and identity never gave me the pause I needed to look inward. I never stopped to understand why I wanted to leave places once I became comfortable. Challenging and snubbing my residency became part of my defiance, and I looked at those who never left places as being stagnant and boring.

Deep down, I was jealous. Jealous of people with roots. Jealous of people that had family nearby to help with date nights and that would make you chicken soup when you were sick. I resented the fact that locals had their home teams and would drape themselves with body paint and jersey numbers. I don't understand the importance of having a connection to someplace you could truly call "home," but I am trying.

I'm trying to embrace the places I am familiar with on a day-to-day basis. The routine treks to drop off and pick up my kids from school are opportunities to ask about their days and not be distracted by new addresses and landmarks. Finding what I need at the grocery stores I frequent right away lets me get on to more important things sooner and not get caught up in impulse buying and spending more time and money. Most importantly, seeing my wife in the same light and situations every day is a blessing that I won't take for granted. She could have easily left, like so many had before, when things got tricky. She could have been too preoccupied with her own world to identify with what I was going through and have the difficult conversations and take the difficult actions to help me. Our address may change, and we may go through some storms now and then, but she is where I want to be. She is my connection to everything good I have in life. Jenny is my home.

But clinging to the narrative that "all is well" contributed to my decline, and I'm trying to find the happy medium where I can identify the things that don't matter and fight for the things that do. It's a balance of being passive and assertive, and it is a constant mental and emotional struggle.

I still suppress things that suck, and I can feel myself revert to the same anger and passive-aggressive behaviors that I used in the past. Nicole suggests that I journal and meditate each day to ground myself and express my frustrations in a healthy, constructive way. For me, a hyperactive, overworked man, I find it more beneficial to go for a walk, scream into a pillow, or piss on a tree to assert my authority over something inanimate.

I KNOW BEST

During my time of self-exploration, self-discovery, and ultimately, self-preservation, I had to spend a lot of time with… well, myself.

It's easy to focus on the exterior to remedy what's not working on the inside. I spent years focusing on my appearance and my career as a form of validation only to find that I eventually grew man tits and lost job after job. My purpose in life was motivated by what I made, not by what I was. Like many men my age, my reward system was based on performance and perseverance. I was never taught that I was good or bad; I was never told when to come home, and aside from after-school specials, I was never told that contemplating suicide was something that only valley girls in their teens had to worry about.

I struggle to find the good in me, and my internal monologue has never been kind. I have to really think about what I like about myself and turn that into a mantra. It's a little new-age and beyond what I was taught, but it's something that therapy has assured me would help. It's not easy to be your "biggest fan," but in the absence of a well-nurtured inner child, positive self-talk is important.

Seeking approval from my parents has been a lifelong struggle, and I still try to find ways to excuse bad behaviors and justify cold shoulders and callous remarks. Becoming my own parent and giving myself structure, love, and discipline has been the hardest obstacle in this journey. It's a constant dilemma of second-guessing and self-doubt that makes me feel absolutely insane.I'm supposed to recognize and nurture my inner child. I'm even supposed to wrap my arms around myself and give me a big hug.

I'm not there yet. Baby steps, you know.

AND FINALLY...FEEL BAD

This last year has been a journey of reflection and dissection. It was a period where my emotional dissociation was held accountable by the compassion of loved ones, the forgiveness of the past, and the healing of self. It was a time to physically remove myself from distractions and focus on what it means to be present and peaceful. I also learned the importance of family and how they can positively (and negatively) define your path and how the societal assumptions of right and wrong can influence your attitude in life.

But the most important takeaway from this trip is knowing it's okay to feel bad. In fact, how can you feel good if you've never felt bad? How can you know what the highs are in life if you've never hit rock bottom? All my rules were attempts to guide my life toward distractions and make sense of things I didn't really want to face.

Going back to Montana was cleansing for my soul and gave me the opportunity to fill a void with positivity and hope. It was learning things firsthand and challenging things and people I thought I knew. It wasn't saying goodbye to my father for my sisters. It wasn't a stab in the back to my mother, and it wasn't the cathartic journey that Jenny thought I was taking. It was me embracing the bad for the first time in my life. It was a connection to pain and the people who caused it. I learned that we often don't heal from past pain and present circumstances. We may never be cured of addictions and broken hearts. We are not saved from poor choices and are prone to good fortune. The majority of us are going to be plagued by pain, and we just have to fight hard. We have to bandage our wounds and fight through expectations, temptations, bad luck, and bears.

We have to endure the wonderful chaos in life that is unique to us and gives us our tragic backstory. We have to learn from our past, be in the present, and do better for our future. We have to know our journey's starting point to know where we want it to end. At its very essence, we all have to know where we are from.

As for me...I'm Montana made.

Garth Gerhart is the writer and illustrator of the comic "Bitterman" in Mad Magazine and the owner of the creative design agency, GerhartInk, LLC. He lives in Maryland with his wife, Jennifer, and his collection of kids: Parker, Gwendolyn, and McKenzie, and his dogs.

Montana Made: A Coming of Middle Age Story is a humorous, brutally honest autobiographical account of Garth Gerhart, a 40-something, rule-abiding family man who finds himself struggling with a past he can't face, a present he can't stand, and a future he can't imagine.

When his estranged father dies, Garth's battle with regret, fear, and anger takes him down a dark path as he reluctantly returns to Montana to lay his father and his past to rest.

Along his journey, Garth discovers truths he'd never known and a family he'd never met. As he gets further from the safe harbor of his former life, he must venture to unexplored places within himself to find his way home.